Good and Bad Times
in a
San Francisco Neighborhood

A History of Potomac Street and Duboce Park

Revised Edition

H. Arlo Nimmo

October Properties
San Francisco

ISBN 978-1534686052

Book design by Cass Brayton
Cover design by Audrey Feely
Cover graphic edges: © CottageArts.net, LLC

Published by

October Properties
San Francisco

To

the past, present, and future residents

of

Potomac Street

Contents

Illustrations

Preface

I T IS FREQUENTLY SAID that San Francisco is a city of neighborhoods. And although every city is a city of neighborhoods, San Francisco is perhaps more so because of its hilly terrain and multi-ethnic population which have resulted in distinctive neighborhoods clustered in valleys, scattered on slopes, and perched atop hills. Thus, the Mission District is home to Latinos, African Americans are gathered in the Western Addition and Bay View-Hunter's Point, several "Chinatowns" dot the cityscape, gays and lesbians claim the Castro as their turf, the Lower and Upper Haight host the counterculture set, and the well-heeled have staked out Pacific Heights and Sea Cliff as their domains. Other neighborhoods are perhaps less well-known, but each is nonetheless distinctive with its own history. Consequently, San Francisco is a colorful mosaic of neighborhood histories which together reveal its multifaceted past.

This book explores the history of Potomac Street and Duboce Park, a short street and a small park in the Lower Haight neighborhood of San Francisco.* It presents that history through two perspectives: one objective and the other subjective. Part One, "History," discusses the park's origin and the beginnings of Potomac Street. It then surveys changes in the neighborhood, especially the street's population, nativity, ethnicity, household composition, occupations, and political affiliation since its founding in 1899 up to 2007. The data utilized include quantitative data such as San Francisco city documents, United States census reports, and newspaper stories as well as qualitative data, such as interviews with longtime residents and my own observations during thirty-five years of residence on the street. Part Two of the book, "Musings and Memories," is a more subjective, recent history of the street and park based on my personal observations as recorded in a journal I kept during my residence on the street from 1972 through 2007. A 2016 Afterword discusses changes in the neighborhood since the original publication of this book in 2007.

---

* This book is a greatly expanded and updated version of a booklet I wrote in 1997 titled *Potomac Street: A Footnote to San Francisco History.*

Several people have helped with this book. First and foremost, I thank Marc Scruggs who lived these many years with me in our home on Potomac Street overlooking Duboce Park. His input into this book has been invaluable in too many ways to enumerate here. I also wish to thank Margaret McElhiney for her assistance as all-around editor in every stage of the production of this book. Thanks to Tanya Joyce for allowing me to reprint her poem "Memorial Piece for Mrs. Smith" in Appendix 6. Neighbors Christina Jobst and Gloria Wilkins shared memories of their longtime residence in the neighborhood. And a very special thanks to Cass Brayton who patiently and cheerfully put up with my changes to his book design and Audrey Feely who was equally patient and cheerful with my changes to her cover design. Also, thanks to Ben Tavernier for his questions and encouragement.

Good and Bad Times
in a
San Francisco Neighborhood

PART ONE

HISTORY

Duboce Park, 1906. *The park became a refugee camp for people displaced by the 1906 earthquake and fire. Such camps filled parks and open spaces throughout San Francisco. Most of the buildings in this photo are still intact. (The Society of California Pioneers Collection)*

The Neighborhood

Located three blocks from Market Street, the major downtown thoroughfare of San Francisco, Duboce Park is a little-known neighborhood of the city. The park, around which the neighborhood clusters, comprises only 4.21 acres of land and is bordered by Steiner Street on the east, Duboce Avenue on the south, Scott Street on the west, and private properties on the north. Three streets, namely Potomac, Pierce, and Carmelita, end in cul-de-sacs at the northern boundary of the park. Pierce Street is a major street that crosses the northern half of the city and ends at Duboce Park, whereas Potomac and Carmelita are each only a half-block long off Waller Street.

The park and the houses between its northern boundary and Waller Street were more recently developed than the surrounding neighborhoods. In 1853, the city passed an ordinance to purchase land for the purpose of building a city hospital. Eventually the entire block bounded by Duboce Avenue, Steiner Street, Waller Street, and Scott Street was purchased by the city for a "reserve for Hospital Purposes."[1] The land surrounding the

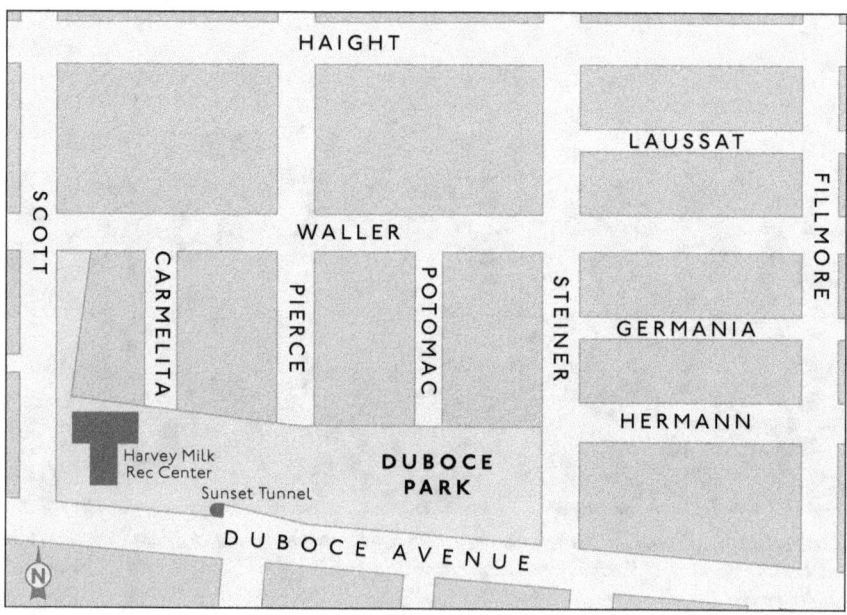

Map of Duboce Park neighborhood.

German Hospital, 1883. *German Hospital opened in 1878 at the corner of Noe Street and Duboce Avenue which was then countryside. This photograph captures a rare San Francisco snowfall that dropped three and a half inches of snow on the city. Home to hospitals throughout its history, this site is currently occupied by California Pacific Medical Center. (Author's Collection)*

hospital lot was developed for residential use while the city planned its hospital. Two private parties, however, put a halt to the plans when they sued the city for part of the hospital land which they claimed was theirs. They won their suit and on May 20, 1869, the present residential land in the block was awarded to them. Other claims were filed for the remaining land (the present park), but they were lost in both the Superior Court and the California Supreme Court in 1897.*

While the city was in court settling claims to its hospital land, the German General Benevolent Society was planning its own hospital in the nearby block bordered by Duboce Avenue, Noe Street, 14th Street, and Castro Street. The cornerstone of the new hospital, appropriately called German Hospital, was laid July 29, 1877 on the "hilly location, studded with trees [which] was much admired and the mild climate lauded" by the attendees.[2] The new hospital opened its doors to the public in February 1878.

For unclear reasons, the city property that was returned to private ownership in 1869 was not developed until the turn of the century. Perhaps the owners were awaiting the outcome of the litigation over the remaining

---

* See Appendix One (page 112) for an outline of the legal history of Duboce Park.

Duboce Park site, circa 1890. *Before Duboce Park was established in 1900, the site was used as a construction company maintenance yard. (San Francisco Public Library Collection)*

hospital land or perhaps the city disallowed development until the litigation was finally resolved in 1897.[3] During this period as the courts debated the fate of the land, the future park was used as a stable, a vegetable garden, a construction company maintenance yard, and a dumping ground for rocks from the Duboce Avenue cut through the hill where the United States Mint now stands.

At the turn of the century, the site of the future park was filled with rocks, ramshackle buildings, and construction equipment. The neighborhood grew tired of the unsightly lot, formed an association called the "New Park Improvement Club," and offered to build a park on the site if the city would remove the debris. The city agreed to do so and on April 13, 1900, the land was dedicated for public park purposes. The club raised $1,500 and the Board of Supervisors appropriated an additional $5,000 to prepare the site.[4] It was cleared of everything but the rocks which were gathered into piles and planted as rock gardens. Ray Olinger, a resident of the neighborhood at the turn of the century, remembered the park's beginnings:

> The property now known as Duboce Park was then covered with rock residue, deposited there by the excavators of the Market and Hermann Street [Duboce Avenue?] cuts, surrounding the property on which the former [present] United States Mint now stands.
>
> The property owners offered the city management a request to build a park on the city-owned, rock strewn land, if the city would remove the debris. The request was granted, and all the property owners in the district contributed to the planting and construction of the new park. Incidentally, the foundation of your building

6

[47-49-51 Potomac Street] was made from some of the smaller rocks which occupied the park site.[5]

On September 9, 1900, at a special ceremony in the "old hospital lot," the plot was designated "Duboce Park," named after Colonel Victor D. Duboce, a veteran of the Philippines War and a recently deceased member of the Board of Supervisors.[6] On September 10, 1900, the *San Francisco Call* carried the following story about the dedication of the park:*

DUBOCE PARK IS NOW FOR THE CITY
Amid Roar of Cannon and Cheers of Crowd
Hero's Memorial is Dedicated

Amid the booming of a small cannon and the cheers of a large concourse of people among whom were the Army and Navy and Olympic parlors of the Native Sons, officers of the First Regiment, N. G. C., and well-known citizens, Duboce Park was formally dedicated yesterday morning.

Shortly after 10 o'clock E. C. Priber, president of the Duboce Park Improvement Club, introduced Mayor Phelan, who in a short speech complemented the club for its work in securing the old "hospital lot"

Duboce Park, 1904. The pre-park site was littered with rocks from the Duboce Avenue cut through the hill where the United States Mint now stands. When the city dedicated the site as a park, neighbors collected the rocks into piles which were then planted as rock gardens. This early photo reveals a dry streambed in the park. (San Francisco Public Library Collection)

---

* See Appendix Two (page 114) for another newspaper account of the Duboce Park dedication ceremonies.

for park purposes. The Mayor spoke feelingly of the late Colonel Duboce and added that in naming the park the people had paid a fitting tribute to the hero's memory. He promised that he would do his utmost to have the $5000 appropriation expected at an early date.

Rabbi Voorsanger, in the absence of Julius Kahn, delivered the dedicatory address. He declared that Supervisor Charles Boxton had done much to carry the project through its many trials to the perpetuation of his comrade's memory. Dr. Voorsanger closed his remarks by saying: "Let us unfurl the banner that Colonel Duboce so nobly defended." Little Elsa Priber at that moment cut the cord which held the flag, and members of the Army and Navy Parlor hoisted Old Glory to the top of the staff amid cheers.

The First Regiment band furnished the music during the ceremonies.[7]

The hospital land that was returned to private ownership was not incorporated into the surrounding Western Addition but rather was declared a separate tract called "Marion Tract." It is unclear when the streets in the new tract were constructed for housing development, but there was a change of mind regarding the names of the two new streets. Pierce Street was simply extended across Waller Street into the new tract. Carmelita and Potomac, however, were new streets that cut mid-block off Waller Street into the new residential area. The "1898 Election Precinct of [the] 37th District Map" shows Carmelita Street as "Primrose Street" while Potomac Street is identified as "Daisy Street." San Francisco Water Department records for seven of the properties on Potomac Street record "Pretoria" as the street name; however, this name is crossed out and "Portola" is written in.* Whether "Pretoria" was once the name of the street or a clerical error is unclear. By the time of the 1900 census, Primrose had become Carmelita Street and Daisy (or Pretoria) was Portola Street. It was not until 1927 that Portola Street was renamed Potomac Street.

The nineteen dwellings originally constructed on Potomac Street are still standing. Of the late Victorian and early Edwardian styles, they lack the ornate facades of the earlier Victorian architecture of San Francisco. The exteriors of five buildings have been altered with stucco and shingles over the years, but they blend into the original architecture and present a harmonious front to the street. Less harmonious are the added fire escapes

---

* San Francisco Water Department records are among the few city documents that survived the earthquake and fire of 1906. The records list the date when water service was first turned on to properties and, consequently, provide approximate dates for the completion of pre-earthquake buildings.

that protrude from two of the buildings. The two buildings at the end of the street, on the corner of Potomac and Waller, have entrances on Waller Street and their orientation is to that street. Consequently, they are excluded from this discussion. The corner building on the west side of the street, however, has a lower unit at the back with an entrance on Potomac Street and therefore is included in this discussion. Cleis Press currently occupies the storefront on this corner, but throughout most of the street's history it was a grocery store. A commercial space once occupied the opposite corner also, but it was converted to residential use in the early part of the last century. Address numbers on the east side of Potomac Street are inconsistent: there is no 58, 62, 78, or 80. Whether this was a clerical error or represents a deviation from the original construction plan is unknown. As most of San Francisco's old residential neighborhoods, the houses are built side-by-side with no space between them.

Potomac Street has wide sidewalks and prior to the advent of the automobile and the installation of garages, most houses had small gardens in front. These gardens are now driveways that lead to basement garages. However, many households have utilized what small garden space remains for flowers and shrubs, and they with sidewalk trees, soften the street. Most houses have back gardens of varying sizes. Potomac Street is narrower than most streets of San Francisco. This, combined with its short length and cul-de-sac, provides an intimacy to the street which results in social interaction among residents as they come and go, sweep their sidewalks, or sit on front steps on warm days.

In 2007, Potomac Street had forty-one residential units. The number of units on the street, however, has varied over the years. Originally there were twelve single family homes of two and three stories; one of these became a duplex and another was converted to a four-plex. Seven buildings were originally constructed as three-flat residences of three and four stories.* One of these buildings has been altered to five living units. Other alterations have occurred over the years: Several flats, as well as some basements, were divided into small apartments during World War II to accommodate the large population that flocked to the city at that time. Most of these were returned to their original uses after the war.

Throughout my residence on the street, a significant difference has always existed between resident property owners and tenants. Probably this has always been the case. In general, property owners are long-term

---

* In San Francisco, a flat is usually defined as a self-contained residential unit that occupies the entire floor of a building. An apartment shares the floor with other living units.

residents who know and interact with one another regularly, whereas ten-ants tend to be short-term residents and interact less frequently with oth-ers on the street. Exceptions occur, of course. Some tenants have lived on the street a very long time and consider themselves as permanent, if not more permanent, as some property owners who have recently moved to the street.

Socializing occurs among Potomac Street residents. Some regularly visit one another's homes for dinners, birthday parties, and other special occasions, such as Christmas open-houses. Children play groups occasion-ally form on the street. Neighborhood-watch groups and park concerns bring residents together at times. And periodically, residents share the grief of neighborhood deaths at funerals.

The section of Haight Street now known as the Lower Haight is the nearest commercial corridor that serves the Potomac Street neighborhood. This three-block stretch is typical of most older neighborhoods of San Francisco where shops such as meat markets, bakeries, grocery stores, res-taurants, drugstores, clothing stores, bookstores, and hardware stores serve the needs of the surrounding blocks and house tenants in the flats and apartments above them. Scattered among the residential blocks and usually located on corners are small "Mom and Pop" grocery stores which stock the daily necessities of nearby residents. As noted, such a store was historically located at the corner of Potomac and Waller streets.

During most of my residency on the street, property ownership has been fairly stable although in recent years home sales have increased as owners capitalized on the great growth in real estate values. Seven households have owned their homes more than thirty years. Of the nineteen buildings on Potomac Street, all but three are currently owner-occupied and one of these is under renovation for conversion to tenants-in-common occupancy.*

1899–1900

In June 1900, when the first Portola Street census was taken, the popu-lation of the sparsely settled street was only twenty-five and only six houses were occupied, namely numbers 56, 60, 63, 64, 65, and 67. According to the San Francisco Water Department records, water was first turned on in these houses in 1899.

The census-taker probably skirted construction debris and empty lots as he counted residents. The street was no doubt abuzz with the sounds of

---

* Tenants-in-common occupancy is when a multi-unit building is owned jointly by several people who each occupy a unit in the building.

10

saws and hammers as well as horse-drawn drays bringing loads of construction materials as houses were being built. Prospective buyers and tenants as
well as neighborhood curiosity-seekers must have added to the lively scene.
The census-taker discovered that four houses contained nuclear families*
and two houses were occupied by married couples without children.† One
family had a "boarder" and a "servant," and one of the couples rented a room
to a fifteen-year-old student boarder.‡ Five houses were owner-occupied
and mortgage-free whereas one house was rented. One household was
headed by Charles H. Olinger (63 Portola Street) and another by George
Moore (56 Portola Street), the two men who developed the street according
to Olinger's daughter:

> A Mr. George Moore, a contractor, and my father [Charles H.
> Olinger] bought all the land on both sides of the street. It was then
> known as Portola Street. Some lots were sold and others were sold
> with the completed buildings, which you can see are of a similar
> pattern.[8]

The two men were professionally qualified to develop the street since
the census reports Olinger as a "lumber dealer" and Moore as a "construction [sic] & builder." Of the twenty-five people living on the street, eleven
were children (eight girls and three boys) who ranged in age from one to
fifteen with a median age of six. All the children were born in the United
States, ten in California. The fourteen adults ranged in age from twenty to
fifty-three with a median age of forty: seven were women and seven were
men. Six of the women were married and one was divorced; six men were
married and one was single. Six of these adults were born in the United
States, four in California. Three were born in English Canada, three in
Germany, one in Ireland, and one in Spain of English parents. The only
woman who claimed a profession was a servant while the male professions included three managerial positions (hotel keeper, lumber dealer, and
builder) and three skilled blue-collar workers (electrician, carpenter, and
machinist). One of the male professions is illegible on the census report.
The race of everyone on the street was "White" and everyone (excluding
three small children) could read, write, and speak English.

---

* A nuclear family is a man and woman married to one another and their children.

† Appendix Three (page 116) lists the people living on Potomac Street in 1900, 1910,
1920, 1930, and 1940 as reported by the U.S. censuses for those years.

‡ The census lists both boarder and lodger but it does not differentiate the two. A traditional distinction is that a boarder sleeps and eats on the premises whereas a lodger
simply sleeps there.

1901 – 1910

By 1903, all but one of the nineteen buildings currently on Portola Street were constructed and occupied. By far the most important event between the censuses of 1900 and 1910 was the 1906 earthquake and fire that destroyed much of San Francisco. The fire stopped only blocks from Portola Street and the residents must have experienced some anxious moments as the flames leapt nearer. The extent of earthquake damage to houses on Portola Street is unknown but many current residents have uncovered old repairs in their homes which they believe date to the 1906 quake. Probably many homes on Portola Street were opened to displaced friends and relatives. A photo from the period (page 3) shows refugees from the quake camped in tents in Duboce Park.

As most of the city, the neighborhood was without water because of broken water mains. Fortunately, nearby German Hospital (now California Pacific Medical Center) had its own wells and shared water with the neighborhood:

> So hospital employees pumped water day and night, filled barrels and tubs with it and trucked it to three locations nearby where, with soldiers standing by to supervise, water was distributed to householders for one hour in the morning, one hour at noon and one hour in the evening. The hospital set up wound dressing stations where outpatients could be treated. Its relief committee collected food, tools and sewing machines which it passed out to the neighbors as basic necessities.[9]

Many people from Portola Street were probably in line for the water, goods, and services distributed by German Hospital. The hospital suffered toppled chimneys which made cooking impossible in its kitchen and the main sewer pipe collapsed creating a sanitation hazard. There was no gas or electricity so surgery was performed "with the aid of a locomotive headlight borrowed from a railroad." The sick and injured began streaming into the hospital and it was soon overcrowded with some five hundred patients who were accommodated in double rows of beds set up in the long hallways.[10]

At the time of the earthquake, a new hospital was under construction on the site of the old one. Needless to say, the construction was halted; the new hospital was not completed until June 1908.[11]

During the first decade of the 20th Century, Portola Street was filled with the languages and probably some of the dress of northern Europe, revealing the birthplaces of a third of the adult population. Some of their jobs, such as harness-making and millinery, reflected the period. Although automobiles were still rare, the little street was probably regularly visited by horse-drawn drays selling ice, milk, coal, fruits and vegetables, and other needs of the residents.

At the time of the 1910 census, the population of Portola Street had grown from twenty-five in 1900 to 149 (seventy-two females and seventy-seven males). Thirty-one households were occupied: eleven were owned (two had mortgages) and the others were rented. Two households from the 1900 census were at the same addresses in 1910. Everyone on the street, except small children, was able to read, write, and speak English. "White" was the race of all residents.

Of the thirty-one households on Portola Street, nine were childless married couples. One of these shared the household with a mother-in-law and two rented rooms to lodgers. Nuclear families living alone comprised seven households. Nuclear families with additional relatives of either spouse accounted for three households. Two nuclear families rented rooms to lodgers, and two related nuclear families shared a household. Two unrelated nuclear families living together were found in two households. Variations of the nuclear family included a man living with his two daughters and a man living with his daughter-in-law and granddaughter. Widows headed five households: three shared the household with a relative or relatives and two operated lodging houses. A total of thirty-three lodgers lived on Portola Street. Two households had live-in servants.

The twenty-four children (eleven girls and thirteen boys) on the street ranged in age from one to seventeen with a median age of eleven. All were born in California, except three who were born elsewhere in the United States and one in "English Australia." Among the 125 adults, ages ranged from eighteen to eighty-five with a median age of thirty-six. Of the sixty-one adult women, seventeen were single, thirty were married, twelve were widows, and two were divorced. Of the sixty-four adult men, twenty-four were single, thirty-five were married, four were widowers, and one was divorced. Forty-seven of these adults were born in California and thirty-seven were born elsewhere in the United States. Of the forty-one foreign-born adults, fifteen were women and twenty-six were men. Thirty-four had northern European origins, namely Ireland (eight), Sweden (eight), England (five), English-speaking Canada (five), Germany (three), Scotland (two), German-Switzerland (one), Norway (one), and Wales (one). Seven identified as "Bohemian Australians" and two as "Yiddish Russians."

Fifty-six men on the street were employed. The majority of them held white-collar jobs, namely two solicitors, two engineers, a dentist, an attorney, a florist, a barber, a tailor, a real estate agent, a draftsman, an optician, a stationery merchant, a property manager, an advertising agent, a hotel clerk, a bookkeeper, a lumber clerk, a railroad clerk, a shoe store clerk, a clothing store clerk, and a secretary. Blue-collar workers included a carpenter, a cabinet-maker, a contractor, an upholsterer, a machinist, a house-painter, a printer, a plumber, a harness-maker, and a boilermaker. One "artist" resided on the street.

Seventeen women held jobs outside their homes: three milliners, three nurses, two clerks, two servants, a bookkeeper, a laundress, a tailor, a rooming-house proprietor, a packer, a saleslady, and a dress-maker.

1911 – 1920

Among the significant events for Portola Street residents between the 1910 and 1920 censuses were the Panama Pacific International Exposition held in the city in 1915, World War I, and the great influenza epidemic of 1918-1919. The Exposition announced to the world that San Francisco had recovered from the earthquake and fire of 1906. Residents of Portola Street probably joined the throngs from California, the nation, and the world who visited the displays in the Marina District. World War I surely affected all members of the little street in one way or another. Some probably had family members who fought in the war while others worked in war-related civilian jobs. Residents of German ancestry probably had mixed feelings about the conflict and felt its barbs in various personal ways. Nearby German Hospital changed its name to the more politically correct Franklin Hospital in 1917.[12] The hospital was filled to capacity with victims of the influenza epidemic that spread worldwide in 1918-1919 killing millions of people. Doubtless some Portola Street residents suffered the disease.

In 1911, the remaining empty lot (82-84-86 Portola Street) on the street was filled with a three story building of small flats.* According to the 1920 census, the Portola Street population remained constant with a total of 149 residents, eighty females and sixty-nine males. Seven households from the 1910 census appeared at the same addresses in 1920; one of these households, the Olingers, had been at the same address (63 Portola) since 1900 and would continue to own property (47-49-51 Portola) on the street until 1955. Only four households were owned (one with a mortgage), down from eleven in 1910. The population was still entirely White and all, except small children, read, wrote, and spoke English.

---

* City records for the building report 1911 as its construction date. However, the address does not appear in the 1920 census.

Thirty-seven households were occupied in 1920. Nuclear families living alone comprised fifteen households and nuclear families with additional relatives of either spouse occupied three households. One nuclear family shared its home with lodgers, another had a boarder, and still another had a live-in housekeeper. Nine households were occupied by childless married couples: one of these rented to a lodger, two shared their space with a mother-in-law, and one accommodated three relatives and a boarder. Two unrelated married couples shared a household. Six widows headed households which they typically shared with other family members or lodgers and boarders. A total of thirteen lodgers and seven boarders lived on the street.

The thirty children (seventeen girls and thirteen boys) on the street were aged two to seventeen with a median age of seven. All were born in California except three who were born elsewhere in the United States. Ages of the 119 adults ranged from eighteen to eighty-four with a median age of forty-two. Of the sixty-three adult women, fifteen were single, thirty-four were married, and fourteen were widows. Of the fifty-six adult men, fifteen were single, thirty-seven were married, two were divorced, and two were widowers. Fifty-one adults were born in California and thirty-eight were born elsewhere in the United States. Of the thirty foreign-born adults, fourteen were men and sixteen were women. Eighteen came from northern Europe, namely Sweden (six), Germany (four), England (four), and Ireland (four). Other birthplaces were Bohemian Australia (six), Estonia (two), Hungary (one), Nova Scotia (one), New Zealand (one), and Australia (one).

The jobs of the Portola Street men in 1920 revealed the same diversity reported a decade earlier. White-collar workers dominated the street and included two doctors, a bookkeeper, an information clerk, a bank teller, a clerk, a mailing clerk, a salesman, an architecture draftsman, a tailor, a paper company manager, an assistant manager of a safe deposit vault, a 2nd ship's officer, an assistant manager of a packing company, a shoe dealer, an auto store manager, a grocery merchant, a grocery proprietor, an engineer, an attorney, and a dentist. A musician was the only artist on the street. Blue-collar workers included three machinists, a woodworker, a glassworker, a safe expert, a concrete contractor, a housepainter, an electrician, an auto-painter, a fireman, an iron works patternmaker, a printer, a suitcase manufacturer, a plasterer, a glazier, a roofer, a laborer, a stevedore, and a porter. Two adult men were students. Nine men owned their own businesses, namely a dentist, a doctor, an attorney, a cement contractor, a suitcase manufacturer, a grocery store proprietor, a grocery store merchant, a glazier, and a shoe dealer. All others were salaried.

Twenty-one women held jobs outside their homes: a librarian, a milliner, a hotel chambermaid, a dressmaker, a boarding house proprietor, a music teacher, a housekeeper, two salesladies, two seamstresses, two nurses, two clerks, two bookkeepers, and four stenographers. The milliner and the music teacher owned their own businesses.

The 1912 *San Francisco Register of Voters* (the earliest one available for Portola Street) reported that of the sixty-eight registered voters, fifty-three (78%) were Republicans, thirteen (19%) were Democrats, and two were Socialists (3%). Of these sixty-eight registered voters, thirty-one were women[13] who first won the right to vote in state elections in 1911. They would have to wait until 1920 before they could vote in national elections.

In 1920, seventy people on Portola Street registered to vote: forty-four (63%) were Republicans, eleven (16%) were Democrats, two (3%) were Socialists, and one (1%) had no party affiliation. Twelve (17%) people declined to state their party affiliation.[14]

1921 – 1930

In August 1927, the residents of Portola Street received a new identity when the name of their street was changed to Potomac Street.[15] The city administrators apparently decided that it was confusing to have both a Portola Drive and a Portola Street named after Gaspar de Portola, the Spaniard who discovered the San Francisco Bay for Spain. The choice of "Potomac" for the new name was perhaps governed by the similarity of syllables and sounds in the two names.

Another memorable event for residents of the street during this decade was the laying of streetcar tracks up Duboce Avenue and through the newly excavated tunnel under Buena Vista hill.* This new line, the N-Judah line, which opened in 1928, provided service to the rapidly expanding residential areas in the western part of the city. This not only gave Potomac Street residents easier access to the area beyond Buena Vista hill, including Ocean Beach, but also gave them another route downtown.[16] Streetcar lines on Haight Street, a block away, and Market Street, three blocks away, provided downtown transportation prior to the opening of the new line.

Potomac Street was still apparently a desirable place to live: Dr. and Mrs. Milton McMurray and their two daughters were listed in the *San Francisco Blue Book* (subtitled "The Fashionable Private Address Directory") at 65 Portola (now Potomac) Street from 1911 to 1927. Probably some of the

---

* Although this tunnel is known in the neighborhood as Sunset Tunnel, it is officially named East Portal.

Construction of Sunset Tunnel, 1926. The N-Judah streetcar line began operating through the Sunset Tunnel under Buena Vista hill in 1928. The new line provided Potomac Street residents an easier access to the western part of the city as well as another option for going downtown. (Author's Collection)

basements were altered during this decade to create the first garages on the street as automobiles became increasingly common. The stock market crash of 1929 doubtless caused concern for Potomac Street investors and would result in even greater grief during the Great Depression in the following decade.

The 1930 Census for Potomac Street is incomplete. The census-taker missed six addresses, namely 46, 49, 59, 72, 77, and 82, and several names on the census form are illegible. Despite these shortcomings, the census none-theless provides insights into the street's residents. The census documents a population of only 109 residents, forty-three women, forty-nine men, and seventeen children. However, if all residents had been counted, most likely the street's 1930 population would approximate the 149 residents reported for both 1910 and 1920.

Of the households reported, fourteen were nuclear families: two of these included in-laws and two others included boarders. Nine households were childless married couples: two shared the household with an in-law and two rented to lodgers. Four households consisted of a parent and child, one of these also included a grandparent and another included a boarder. A brother and sister comprised a household in two instances. Nine people on the street were "lodgers," three were "roomers," and one was a "boarder."

Duboce Park, 1929. *This photo reveals Duboce Park before it was invaded by the Harvey Milk Recreation Center, the basketball court, and the playground – and before automobiles clogged the streets. (San Francisco Public Library Collection)*

Two unmarried adults (a man and a woman) rented rooms in their respective flats to boarders. The compositions of the six uncounted households are unknown but were probably similar to the counted ones.

The occupations of the 1930 Potomac Street residents were almost equally divided between white-collar workers (twenty-three) and blue-collar workers (twenty-one). Jobs for the men included banker, chauffeur, broker, cabinet maker, carpenter, glass-packer, drayman, stevedore, bookkeeper, restaurant manager, taxi driver, mail carrier, cooper, painter, clerk, engineer, and electrical salesman. The jobs of the nine women who worked outside their homes included stenographer, teacher, tailor, nurse, bookkeeper, real estate agent, dressmaker, and factory worker.

According to the census, twenty-four people rented their homes and eight owned them. The 1930 census requested data on monthly rents paid by tenants as well as the market-value of the owner-occupied properties. Rents for single-family homes ranged from $21.50 to $30 whereas rents for flats ranged from $40 to $55, probably with the understanding that rooms would be sublet to boarders and lodgers. Values of single family homes ranged from $3,000 (69 Potomac Street) to $7,000 (65 Potomac Street). Only two buildings of flats were evaluated: 50-52-54 Potomac was valued at $8,500 and 53-55-57 Potomac at $10,000. This census also inquired about radio-ownership and reported that twelve of the thirty households owned radios.

The ethnic character of the street had changed little since the 1920 census: everyone identified as "White," except one woman who identified as "Sp," presumably Spaniard. Of the ninety-two adults counted in the incomplete 1930 census, forty-one were born in California and twenty-seven were born elsewhere in the United States. Twenty-four adults were foreign-born, almost all from northern Europe: England (7), Czechoslovakia (4), Germany (2), English Canada (2), Scotland (2), Norway (1), Denmark (1), Holland (1), South Africa (1), Ireland (1), Austria (1), and Belgium (1). All adults on the street could speak, read, and write English. All children were American-born.

The 1930 *San Francisco Register of Voters* reveals that political party affiliation on Potomac Street had changed little since 1920. The majority of the thirty-one men on the voting register were white-collar workers, but their predominance perhaps reflects a greater tendency for this class to vote rather than a majority on the street. Twenty women registered to vote. Thirty-six (71%) of the Potomac Street voters were Republicans, twelve (23%) were Democrats, one (2%) was a Socialist, and two (4%) declined to state their party affiliation.[17]

1931 – 1940

During the 1930s, the Great Depression was the major crisis for San Francisco as well as the nation. No record reveals how many people on Potomac Street lost their jobs at this time, but one longtime resident of the neighborhood remembered the hard times by the number of homeless people camped out in Duboce Park:

> St. Joseph's Hospital, several blocks away, handed out free food to the hungry and these poor unfortunates could be seen shedding their overnight blankets in the park and making the uphill walk to the hospital for their daily meal.[18]

The dedication of the new United States Mint in 1937, only two blocks away on Hermann Street, must have presented some irony as well as a spate of jokes during those bleak days. The *San Francisco Chronicle* carried a story about the movement of precious metal from the old mint to the new one on May 13:

Sunset Tunnel, 1935. *An N-Judah streetcar entering Sunset Tunnel at Duboce Park. (Author's Collection)*

More than 1,000 tons of precious metal, valued at $595 million, moved yesterday from the old to the new U.S. Mint in San Francisco. The transfer was made under heavy police and U.S. Secret Service protection.

The metal – a half-billion dollars worth of gold bars and $95 million worth of silver bars – was moved in post office trucks. The trucks sped, one at a time, from the grimy old Mint building at Fifth and Mission to the new at Market Street and Duboce Avenue, under convoy of two police radio cars each. While elaborate precautions were taken, there was little fear of even the most daring gangster attempting a holdup. Each bar weighs 75 pounds.

In the new mint, the gold and silver will be placed in two large vaults guarded by 22-ton doors with time locks and two combination locks each. The vaults have walls of reinforced concrete 2 feet thick, and the mint itself is built on a hill of solid rock.[19]

Ethnic identification was still strong in the area during this period. A man who lived near Haight Street during the 1930s remembered that membership in the neighborhood gangs of boys was usually based on ethnicity. He said the ethnicity of the area was primarily northern European, his own being Russian. The 1940 Census verifies his recollection. Of the 125 people living on Potomac Street, thirty-six were foreign-born, all of whom were northern European except five (Cuba, Egypt, Hawaii, San Salvador and Turkey). All stated their race as "white." Of those who provided their occupations, thirty-eight were blue collar workers, twenty were white collar workers, and six were retired.

According to the Census, the highest rent ($50) on the street was the flat at 51 Potomac Street; other rents ranged from $15 (44 Potomac) to $37.50 (49 Potomac). Property value estimates ranged from $3,500 (59 Potomac) to $10,000 (53-57 Potomac). 52 Potomac was assigned a low value of $1,650.

At the end of the decade, a mini-historical event happened at 51 Potomac Street. Mrs. Zilpa Oram, who rented rooms in her large flat, became concerned about the drinking problem of one of her roomers. She heard about the newly formed Alcoholics Anonymous in New York City and wrote to the organization for information about its program. AA responded and Mrs. Oram encouraged her roomer to host the first Alcoholics Anonymous meeting west of the Rocky Mountains. This meeting was held in the kitchen of 51 Potomac Street in December 1939.[20]

In 1940, ninety-one Potomac Street residents registered to vote. For the first time, blue-collar workers dominated the voting register. This may reflect a change in the composition of the street, or it may reflect the politically sensitive times which brought more blue-collar workers to the polls. Only thirteen of the forty-three registered male voters held white-collar jobs: five clerks, two salesmen, a pianist, a manager, a superintendent, an engineer, a dietitian, a merchant, and a physician. The twenty-five blue-collar workers included two cooks, two laborers, two roofers, a longshoreman, a carpenter, a baker, a stevedore, a butcher, a chauffeur, a janitor, a mechanic, a switchman, a jobber, an electrician, a shoemaker, a motorman, a machinist, a conductor, a houseman, a lineman, a foundry-worker, and a laundry-worker. Four men were retired.

Of the forty-eight women registered to vote, thirty-three were housewives. Those who worked outside the home included four clerks, three nurses, a waitress, a seamstress, a deaconess, a bookkeeper, a solicitor, a student, and a machine operator. One was retired.

A significant shift in political affiliation occurred on Potomac Street between 1930 and 1940. As in most of the United States during the Great Depression, the political hopes of Potomac Street were pinned to the Democratic Party's New Deal. In the past, Republicans dominated the street, but in 1940, sixty-six (73%) of the residents were Democrats, twenty-one (23%) were Republicans, and four (4%) declined to state a party affiliation.[21] This preponderance of Democrats on the street would continue to the present.

1941 – 1950

The 1940s were defined by World War II for Potomac Street residents. San Francisco became an important staging port for troops and equipment destined for the Pacific warfronts. Shipyards and factories at Hunter's Point, Alameda, Richmond, and other parts of the Bay Area geared up for the war effort and attracted civilian employees from throughout the United States. As people moved to San Francisco for jobs and to see loved ones off to the war fronts (and sometimes welcome them home) housing in the city became critical. Every available space was rented as code enforcements were seemingly ignored. Potomac Street probably reflected what was happening throughout much of the city. Most of the large flats were divided into smaller units, and some basements were divided into rooms for rent. Virtually all twenty-two rooms in the building at 47-49-51 Potomac were rented out as "housekeeping units" to individuals, couples, and possibly even families. Similar subdivision occurred elsewhere on the street to meet the housing shortage. No figures exist for the number of people who lived on the street during this time, but it probably reached an all-time high, as did the overall population of San Francisco. Some windows on the street doubtless displayed stars for family members serving in the armed forces. And doubtless some households suffered the loss of loved ones in the conflict.

As much of the nation, Potomac Street residents turned backyards into "Victory gardens" to compensate for food shortages brought on by the war. In August 1943, these shortages were eased when a farmers' market was

Duboce Park, 1945. *This view of the park from Scott Street before the construction of the Harvey Milk Recreation Center reveals the attractive landscaping the park once hosted. (San Francisco Public Library Collection)*

Duboce Park, 1945. *An N-Judah streetcar enters the Sunset Tunnel in this photograph of a beautifully landscaped Duboce Park. (San Francisco Public Library Collection)*

established on the nearby empty lot at Duboce Avenue and Church Street where the Safeway store currently stands. Because of wartime shortages, canneries had insufficient sugar for canning farm produce and farmers brought their surplus crops to the city to sell directly to residents. A huge success, the market was initially managed by the farmers themselves as the "Farmers' Free Market," but a year later, the city assumed its management. In 1947, the market moved to its present location on Alemany Boulevard.[22]

Because of the seventy-two year seal on certain U.S. census data, no relevant Potomac Street census figures are currently available for 1950 and subsequent years. Consequently, other sources must be tapped.

The proportion of blue- and white-collar workers on Potomac Street changed somewhat during World War II. In 1944, the *San Francisco Register of Voters* (the last register to list occupations) reveals that the Potomac men were still almost equally divided between white-collar and blue-collar workers. The eighteen white-collar workers included a manager, a dietitian, a merchant, an inspector, a nurse, two salesmen, four clerks, and seven engineers. The large number of engineers is puzzling and may be related to the war effort. The twenty-four blue-collar workers included a letter carrier, a mechanic, a baker, a soldier, a janitor, a pipe-fitter, an electrician, a laborer, a painter, a teamster, a cook, a shoemaker, a longshoreman, a motorman, a conductor, a houseman, a laundry worker, an officer, a sailor, two stevedores, and two warehousemen. Two men were retired.

Of the thirty-nine women listed in the 1944 *Register*, the majority (twenty-one) were housewives. Those who worked outside the home included a teacher, a stenographer, a secretary, a nurse's aide, a musician, a bookkeeper, a driver, two operators, three nurses, and six clerks.

In 1944, Democrats accounted for fifty-six (68%) residents while Republicans were represented by twenty-two (27%). Four residents (5%) declined to state their party affiliation.[23] By 1950, the political balance had changed somewhat: fifty-seven (73%) were Democrats, eighteen (23%) were Republicans, two (3%) belonged to a party identified as "IPR," and one (1%) gave no party affiliation.[24]

1951 – 1970

In the early 1950s, nearby Haight Street was still a thriving commercial corridor which served most needs of Potomac Street. A long-time resident remembered a well-stocked drug store, a popular bakery that baked its own bread and gave cookies to patrons' children, a meat market that cut meat to order, a branch of the Bank of America, and the Mid-Town Theater that screened movies after they exhausted downtown venues.

But winds of change were beginning to blow down Potomac Street. Between its origins in 1899 and the beginning of World War II, the street had altered little in terms of ethnic, economic, and household compositions. However, the ethnic composition of San Francisco began changing during the war as large numbers of African Americans from the southern states were attracted to wartime jobs in the Bay Area. Initially segregated in the Western Addition and Hunter's Point, the newcomers would have ramifications for Potomac Street in succeeding decades. The first non-White family to move to Potomac Street was a Filipino family that arrived in the late 1940s. In the early 1950s, a Black family moved into one of the flats on the street. Others followed and by the end of the decade, three households were occupied by Filipinos and probably eight households were Black. As non-Whites moved to the street, the familiar exodus of White residents followed. A longtime resident of the street remembered that her White neighbors sold their home because they did not want to live near Blacks. Not all Whites left, however, and a core of homeowners remained on the street throughout the hard times that followed.

Ed Diala fondly remembered his childhood days when his Filipino family lived on Potomac Street during the 1950s:

> Our family lived at 59 Potomac St. from 1953-1959. We were close to the park. I loved the 2 wide, stone steps that led into the park; cars were always parked there but they were a part of the scenery. I remember when my father had the house painted and it was a pretty big job. The steps leading up to the front door were magnificent: gray and pink granite. We were one of the few homes on the "dead end" (now called a cul-de-sac) to have a small garden in front with side gate. Looking back, I realize how fortunate we were to have grown up in a great Victorian house with so much room and space . . .

24

We had a great time growing up there: it was like a scene out of Westside Story with Hispanic/Filipino "crooners" standing at the corners singing. There was racial tension amongst the different ethnic groups as you can imagine but the size of the groups was manageable.

During the late 1950's with much change coming, the street was very international in culture. I remember a dashing couple from England who lived across the street; their daughter (Virginia) was a few years older than me but she and my late sister taught me how to ride a bike. Her father drove a little English sports car ... a red Austin Healy, I think. Our neighbor to our right was from Jamaica who was always smiling and my brother used to call him "Baldy." Our neighbor to our left was a little old Italian lady and her cousin or aunt lived next door to her. Their homes always appeared to be freshly painted.

We weren't allowed to go past the corner onto Waller St. On the corner was our little grocery store where everyone bought groceries. I started my comic book collection from there . . . Next to this was the Laundromat which always seemed full but was always being vandalized.[25]

One of the memorable Potomac Street events in the early 1950s for one resident was a spectacular fire in the large building (47-49-51 Potomac) at the end of the street on the park. The fire destroyed much of the roof and trapped an elderly woman in the top floor. A fireman on a long extension ladder rescued her to the applause of onlookers in the park.

The first violence on the street, as recalled by another resident, was the murder of a Latino man who operated a small grocery store at the corner of Potomac and Waller Street. He was shot during a holdup in the late 1950s, the first of many murders that would disturb the neighborhood in subsequent years.

One of the unfortunate events of this decade was the construction in 1957 of the large recreation building, now known as the Harvey Milk Recreation Center, at the west end of Duboce Park.[26] A more concerned neighborhood would have blocked the construction of the oversized building, but apparently few residents were concerned about its encroachment into the park's green space.

In 1962, a *San Francisco Chronicle* writer visited the Duboce Park neighborhood and was impressed by what she saw:

> Duboce Park, a three-block long strip of airy green at the base of Buena Vista Hill, is a much-used neighborhood public yard, a welcome-mat ushering the N car into Sunset tunnel. It may also be one of those unsuspected blessings the City has yet to count at full value.

She noted that the park and its perimeters fulfilled urban scholar Jane Jacobs' four conditions for an urban environment, namely "multiple uses, short blocks, varied buildings and dense population." She further noted that "the short streets that terminate at the park on the north side, and the houses that face it directly" provide "eyes on the street . . . a greater safety factor than any police patrol." She predicted that "Duboce Park may wake up the day after tomorrow to find itself as fashionable as Telegraph Hill."[27] Her prediction may eventually prove true, but the neighborhood faced some very tough decades before it would become "fashionable."

The construction of public housing projects on nearby Haight Street in 1963 contributed to the deterioration of the neighborhood. Two blocks of San Francisco's famed Victorian buildings were bulldozed to build grim, prison-like structures to house the poor of the city, primarily Blacks. The nearest of these was about four blocks from Potomac Street. During the 1960s, block after block of the Black community in the Western Addition near Civic Center, one of the city's most intact Victorian neighborhoods, was razed for more public housing. Some of this displaced community sought housing in the Lower Haight. As White-owned businesses on Haight Street departed, they were replaced with Black businesses that eventually became overshadowed by a plethora of bars, clubs, and second-hand stores.

The movement of Blacks into Potomac Street continued as absentee landlords allowed their buildings to deteriorate. In addition to Blacks, young White "hippies," the overflow from the Haight-Ashbury neighborhood, also moved to the street. As the street fell into disrepair, so did Duboce Park. The city provided minimal maintenance and much of the grass died. Discarded syringes and needles of drug-users became a concern to mothers whose children played in the park. Neighborhood children routinely broke abandoned beer and wine bottles on sidewalks already littered with broken glass. Igniting overflowing garbage cans was another of their favorite pastimes.

One of the early Black Panther rallies was held on the steps of 47 Potomac Street in the late 1960s. The crowd spilled over into Duboce Park. Also during this period, a minor luminary of the times stayed on the street. African American singer Juanita Hall, known for her Broadway and film portrayals of "Bloody Mary" in the musical *South Pacific*, stayed with a friend who lived at 51 Potomac while she performed in a downtown club. The limousine that picked her up and returned her nightly caused considerable stir on the street.

At the end of the 1960s, the neighborhood was forever altered by the demolition of the handsome brick buildings of Franklin Hospital. On the wooded site of the old hospital was erected the Ralph K. Davies Medical Center (now known as California Pacific Medical Center), three multi-storied concrete blocks that filled the site and dwarfed the surrounding neighborhood residences.

The Haight Street shopping corridor continued to deteriorate as its businesses were increasingly overshadowed by bars and clubs. Haight-Fillmore became one of the most infamous intersections of the city with pushers and pimps offering drugs and sex to the crowds that filled the sidewalks. The intersection was so feared that the bus stop was moved because passengers refused to get off at that stop. Many taxi drivers declined to enter the area because of its lurid reputation.

Despite the disturbing changes on their little street and in their neighborhood, however, many of the old time Potomac homeowners remained, especially the Filipino and Black families who bought homes there in the early 1950s. A small core of Whites stayed on also.

During the early 1970s, 49 Potomac Street was occupied by the Angels of Light, an offshoot of the legendary Cockettes, a counterculture music group of drag queens and "hippies" spawned during the flowerchild era of Haight-Ashbury. A friend of the group remembered one of their parties that got out of hand and resulted in a confrontation with the police.

> Adrian, Crown Prince of Westphalia, and heir to the throne of the Holy Roman Empire, had taken residence at the Potomac St. house. It was bordered on the south side by Duboce Park, stronghold of adolescent and pre-adolescent Black Bandit children who inhabited the surrounding streets in the declining Victorians that filled the pre gentrification era Fillmore District. Potomac was only steps away from the dreaded Haight/Fillmore intersection. It was a real trip waiting for the Muni at that corner. Across the street from the house, also the last house on the street, bordering by this green space on the face of Black Fillmore was the Mukluk Manor, a bunch of maddened heteros, homos, food conspiracy types who prowled the corridor between Haight St and the meetings places south of Market.
>
> Grasshopper had 49 Potomac filled with antique and near antique kitsch items perfectly coordinated with the always present KMPX filling all your senses with the good music, and sometimes very bad taste of a bygone era.
>
> There was no reason for a party other than a need for some extraordinary overindulgence in a vast array of drugs, alcohol and immoral, amoral life and sex styles that brought out Angels, near

Angels, and camp followers that Mitzi knew and traded with. There was Preston ... booze, Adrian ... booze, Tommy Nevin almost drafted into rolling joints full time with Mitzi helping; along with close to 50 other assorted Aquarians. Preston, tall as she was, always insisted on wearing the largest headdress. Though she was not an official Angel of Life [sic], she was included, if only for visual effect. She was aggressive. Tommy Nevin titled her "Preston the instigator". On this day like many others it was pink chiffon. I think he called it the "mamer". So short, that on Preston it was almost a tutu. A moderate, tasteful dash of glitter completed her outfit. Mercedes masqueraded as a bimbo from 1949 in a flowered house dress and a hat from St Vincent de Paul. She matched the fruit wall sconces and ivy wallpaper that confused the time space senses of all who entered. Mercedes was taking a wine collection (her usual way of getting booze for a party). Very little cash actually went to booze however, and most went to administration personnel (Mercedes).

The day was cool, but the coolness soon melted as the beer and cups of assorted hallucinogens mixed with the costumes and gender fuck outfits of the band of love children left behind after the fall of the Haight. The two houses stood as the pillars of Hercules at the end of Potomac St., guarding access to Duboce Park. Locals wishing to visit this green literally had to cross the traffic back and forth between the two beaming citadels. The black children saw an opportunity to breach the normally secure homes. The black, white, glitter combo got out of hand by mid afternoon, with Adrian chasing the black children, and Preston defying innocent passers by. The arrival of several squad cars inflamed the revelers into a confrontation. Royal leaders Preston and Adrian hurling insults and assorted physical objects at the marauding gendarmes, and the ubiquitous black kids on the fringe. They (cops) charged, Adrian leaped over a bush, and Preston flew through the door, tossing her headdress to Mitzi, with the cops twenty feet behind her, flew up the stairs and in the door. Up the stairs, to the drag closet she dashed, dove in and covered herself with fabric, both matching and contrasting, and escaped. The police brushed aside the innocent Mitzi: they attempted to catch the fleeing drag queen. The appearance and aura of Grasshopper's period forties home sufficiently confused these guardians of justice, so when they opened the drag closet door they saw nothing but multicolored rags and veils and assorted drag items. Not wishing to touch anything in there, they didn't look under the first level, where the six foot two Preston lay silently. They lectured anyone who might listen, and withdrew for the afternoon.[28]

1971 – 1980

Probably no decade began less promising for Potomac Street than that of 1970. Times had never been so bad for the little street. Many of its buildings were deteriorated. Three abandoned units with broken windows and doors were occupied by vagrants. Buildings throughout the neighborhood were abandoned and/or unoccupied because of fire damage. Two units on Potomac Street and one at the corner of Potomac and Waller were houses of prostitution. Open drug-dealing was common on the street and in the park which increasingly became a hangout for derelicts and winos. Murders and muggings were routine events in the neighborhood. Nearby Laussat Street was locally known as "Blood Alley" because of the many killings that occurred there. Hookers on the street held a "Laussat Street Fair" one summer and later when one of their prominent pimps was killed, his funeral filled the street with pimps and prostitutes from throughout the Bay Area.

But despite the conditions of the neighborhood and its unsavory reputation, the majority of the population plugged away at jobs to make ends meet. The park was always filled with children when they were not in school. Late afternoon football games were a year-round, daily activity in the lower end of the park. The basketball court at the upper end was seldom unoccupied and nearby lights allowed games to run well into the night. The dilapidated play equipment attracted the younger set. Virtually all the young people in the park were Black. White families with children of school age had long ago left the neighborhood, and the few Asian families seldom allowed their children to play away from home.

In early 1970, the neighborhood had a large enough Black population to convince the city that a model African village was an appropriate addition to the park. According to a newspaper article:

> It [the village] "will educate the children who use it to their cultural heritage through art and play." The village is the end result of a year's vigorous campaigning by the 500 members of the Fair Play Association of Duboce Park, who organized to obtain play equipment for the children of the area. They also succeeded in having the first, fulltime Black playground director assigned to the park.[29]

The village was apparently never built. There was no evidence of it when I arrived in the neighborhood in 1972, and older residents have no recollection of it. In August 1970, the same neighborhood group that sought the African village was successful in installing "safety fencing" along the section of the park near the streetcar tracks that enter Sunset Tunnel.[30] The cyclone fence was subsequently removed when the park was renovated in 1979.

Two events that caught national attention in 1974 touched Potomac Street. During the Patty Hearst kidnapping episode, rumors were rampant throughout the city of her whereabouts. Some claimed she was being held in the Duboce Park neighborhood, although it was never verified. Some Potomac Street residents took advantage of the free food distributed at the nearby Safeway store which Hearst's captors dictated as part of the terms of her release. The infamous "Zebra" killings gave Potomac Street residents concern also. A small group of young Blacks was randomly shoot-

Potomac Street, 1974. The front of 44–46–48 Potomac Street (right) was "modernized" in the 1960s. The building was restored to its original design in the 1970s. (Author's Collection)

ing Whites on the San Francisco streets in early 1974. Such a shooting occurred a few blocks from Potomac Street and increased racial tensions in the neighborhood until the perpetrators were apprehended.

A former San Francisco police officer remembered the crime-ridden Lower Haight neighborhood in the mid-1970s:

> I was a police officer there 35 years ago, the bar at Haight and Fillmore was called the Giant Glass, then Hank's 500 Club, the beat man walked in to make bar checks and you could hear objects hitting the floor as people were hurrying, emptying their pockets of whatever contraband they may have been holding, we would turn the lights up and find guns, knives misc drugs and nobody knew where it came from. There was a photography school in the area [Duboce Park] and at least two or three times a week you could count on someone being mugged or robbed at gun or knifepoint, it was unsafe for females to be walking alone, the area had one of the highest rape incidents, there were shootings and murders almost on a daily basis. We would respond to bogus calls only to be pelted with rocks and bottles or worse. At the corner of Carmelita and Waller a police officer was shot in the back of the head, murdered! he was towing an abandoned vehicle.[31]

The neighborhood was alarmed in March 1975 when sticks of dynamite were found in the Sunset Tunnel near the park entrance. Streetcars were backed up on Duboce Avenue for several hours until the tunnel was deemed safe. Investigators speculated that the explosives probably dated to the tunnel's construction in the late 1920s.[32]

Three months later in mid-June, the neighborhood once again had cause for alarm when a spectacular, wind-whipped fire burned nine buildings – two on Scott Street, two on Haight Street, and five on Waller Street. The night-time fire started in a small rear apartment on Scott Street and quickly spread to other buildings. Strong winds sent flaming embers throughout the neighborhood and property-owners, including several on Potomac Street, sprayed their roofs to douse the embers that alighted. Three-hundred firemen with sixty-three pieces of equipment battled the four-alarm blaze that attracted hundreds of spectators from the neighborhood. Twenty-five families were displaced, but fortunately no lives were lost. It was later determined the cause of the fire was arson.[33]

In the mid-1970s, once again Potomac Street and its environs began to change. As was happening elsewhere in America, young Whites were discovering the old neighborhoods of the inner city. Many of the deteriorated neighborhoods in the Western Addition contained some of the finest Victorian architecture in San Francisco. Young Whites, some of them

Duboce Park, 1976. *A view of the park from the Harvey Milk Recreation Center before it was renovated in 1979. (Author's Collection)*

gay men, began buying the rundown properties that no one else wanted. A federally sponsored, low-interest loan renovation program had successfully transformed the residential district between Duboce Park and Market Street (the so-called "Duboce Triangle") from rundown tenements to one of the desirable neighborhoods of the city. A few shrewd investors realized that the north side of the park (the Potomac Street neighborhood) would be one of the next areas to go. These few tentative investors bought some of the derelict properties on Potomac and nearby streets. Before long, little pockets of brightly painted, renovated buildings dotted the neighborhood. Others followed, and as a new generation with an appreciation for the old buildings and less concern about having Black neighbors moved into the area, a real estate boom began in San Francisco which has not yet stopped. In the mid-1970s, real estate prices began skyrocketing. Potomac Street remained relatively affordable because of the neighborhood's reputation. Increasingly, however, people who could not afford property in other parts of San Francisco began purchasing in the Potomac Street neighborhood.

The commercial corridor of Haight Street lagged behind the changing neighborhood and many businesses still catered largely to the Blacks from the nearby projects which halted property sales and renovations within a block or so of their boundaries. Newcomers to the area avoided Haight Street and went elsewhere for their shopping needs.

In late 1977, one of the city's largest drug busts happened on Haight Street. In early November, the entire 500 block of Haight was invaded by police and undercover men in cars, motorcycles, and on foot. A police lieutenant said the block was chosen for the raid because it had "the heaviest concentration of narcotic pushers in the city." He claimed that on a typical day "50 pushers were selling more than $5000 worth of heroin to customers from all parts of San Francisco and the Bay Area."[34] The raid, planned for many months, was described by a *San Francisco Chronicle* reporter:

> Police sealed off the 500 block of Haight street in the Fillmore district – reputedly the easiest place to buy heroin in Northern California – and arrested 54 people yesterday, most on drug related charges.
>
> At 12:04 p.m., police cars and motorcycles squealed to a stop at each end of the quiet block between Fillmore and Steiner streets. Instantly, undercover officers – black and white, men and women – materialized from doorways, tawdry stores and parked cars, pinning badges on their civilian clothing. They were joined by platoons of uniformed officers, most carrying riot sticks and wearing jumpsuits and plastic helmets, who trotted smartly onto Haight street from the blocked intersections. Together, the 50 uniformed officers and undercover agents herded more than 100 people into the foyer of an abandoned movie house. . . . The raid, which initially netted 49 suspects, occurred so suddenly that seven cars and three trucks – not counting four unmarked cars used by the plainclothes officers – were trapped on the block until they were finally moved out shortly after 1 p.m.
>
> Later, police returned to the scene to arrest five more people on charges of possessing heroin for sale, raising the total number of arrests to 54.[35]

Although many arrests were made, before long the illicit flow of drugs returned to the street. A year later, it was still considered a dangerous area as reported in a news story that revealed crime statistics for the Haight-Fillmore neighborhood:

> In the past year [1977], more than 800 major [Haight-Fillmore] neighborhood incidents have been reported to the police, or about 2½ incidents a day. Of these, more than 400 were classified as major crimes. They included seven rapes, 32 strong-arm robberies, 25 other robberies, 45 aggravated assaults, 57 residential burglaries, 50 auto thefts and one homicide. These statistics do not include other incidents such as narcotics arrests, which are classified separately. But a city report on narcotics offenses states that in February 1978, 32.5% of the city's total occurred in the Northern Station's district, which

Renovation of Duboce Park, 1979. *The playground was moved, walkways were reconfigured, a hill was created near the present playground, and many trees were planted during this poorly planned renovation of the park. Most trees died and it took years for the grass to re-establish itself. (Author's Collection)*

is only one of the city's nine police precincts. Most of the Northern Station's total, which is by far the city's highest, can be directly traced to the Haight-Fillmore area, specifically the 500 block of Haight Street.[36]

Several news stories during the late 1970s expressed concern that the Lower Haight might be overtaken by gays since they were the most evident renovators of many derelict Victorian buildings.[37] Some of the stories were tinged with homophobia, others were blatantly homophobic. Although many gays moved to the area during this period, they were never a dominant presence but they were often blamed for displacing Black residents. In 1979, a gay man predicted that the 500 block of Haight Street would someday be an "inner city suburb of quiche stores, coffeehouses, bars and boutiques fancier than upper Haight Street." He further speculated that the building he owned at 500 Haight Street which he bought for $250,000 would someday be worth three million dollars.[38] His predictions were eventually borne out.

Potomac Street's population was diverse during the 1970s. In 1972, the street had twenty-four Black households, eleven White, four Filipino American, one Japanese American, and one Black/White.* Of these households, six were nuclear families, six were childless married couples, four were straight males living alone, four were widows living alone, three were gay couples, and two were extended families. Other households included a married couple with a boarder, a gay man, a group of unmarried straights, and two straight women. Three units were unoccupied at the time of the census and the composition of six households was unreported.

In the late 1970s, the street's population was perhaps as diverse as it has ever been. Young White professionals lived next door to welfare recipients. Latter-day hippies eked out lives by whatever means possible while next door elderly White widows collected pension and social security checks. Gays and lesbians neighbored yuppie couples and middle class Blacks. Every other person on the street seemed to be an artist of one sort or another. Despite its great diversity, it was for the most part a harmonious street, thanks to some of the gregarious newcomers.

But it was still a tough neighborhood. In 1976, a *San Francisco Examiner* columnist wrote about the Lower Haight which he called "Mint Hill," the area bounded by Buchanan, Scott, Duboce, and Oak streets:

> For the time being, Mint Hill is the most feared neighborhood in San Francisco. Killing thy neighbor comes easy. It is difficult to get a cab to come to Mint Hill. One landlady had 15 break-ins in two months and sold out. That is one Mint Hill. The other Mint Hill is the one which is close to downtown and has some of the prettiest and least expensive available buildings in San Francisco. The other Mint Hill is being invaded by various investors – gay whites with money, mostly – who have the time and the taste to change this place from a crime-ridden corner to a neighborhood with style and class. "You see a guy paying out more than $3000 for a paint job," [said one resident], "you know he ain't messing around."[39]

A year later, the area had not improved much according to a *San Francisco Bay Guardian* reporter:

> [T]he police call the 500 block of Haight Street the most crime-ridden stretch in the city. Almost daily, major violent crimes are committed on the block. Shootings, beatings and stabbings are

---

* During the thirty-five years I have lived on Potomac Street, I have periodically taken informal censuses of the ethnicity and household composition of the street. The data for ethnicity and household composition from 1972 through 2007 are from those censuses.

almost routine. The apparent reason is smack: heroin pushers blatantly ply their trade on the street, in broad daylight as well as night. And the street is usually full of junkies, pushers, pimps and prostitutes. It's a harsh world, reflecting the worst of San Francisco's black ghettos.[40]

Despite the crime-ridden Haight Street corridor, outsiders moved into the neighborhood. Property renovation continued and real estate prices climbed. As the neighborhood changed, the city decided to improve Duboce Park. In 1976, $200,000 was appropriated to renovate the park but the work did not begin until 1979. A new basketball court and playground were constructed at the upper end of the park while the lower area was scraped of soil and landscaped with new walkways and even a new hill. Old trees were saved and over a hundred new ones were planted. Intentions were good, but the results were not entirely successful. The removal of the top soil inhibited the establishment of new grass, and bare spots continue to dot the park. The new trees were chosen with little concern for their suitability to the park environment and most of them died. A new underground sprinkler system has been plagued with problems since its installation.

New streetcar tracks were laid on Duboce Avenue as part of the new Municipal Railway system in the late 1970s. The sleek new orange and white cars on the new tracks added to the revitalization of the neighborhood, although many residents bemoaned the passing of the familiar old green cars and regretted the vibrations from the heavy new ones.

1981–2000

In June 1980, the Duboce Park neighborhood made the local newspapers when residents discovered that a controversial herbicide suspected of posing risks to human health was sprayed on the park. Residents of the street, especially dog-owners and parents with children who played in the park, protested its use. Park officials posted warning signs and heavily watered the park to dilute the solution.[41]

In the early 1980s, Potomac Street experienced its first AIDS death. Others were to follow. The death of neighbors personalized the disease for many of the street's residents, as it did for most San Franciscans.

Perhaps the most significant event of this decade was the change in the commercial section of nearby Haight Street. After lagging behind the surrounding neighborhood, the street began attracting businesses in the mid-1980s, including a produce store, a drug store, a bookstore, a pizza parlor, a meat market, and several restaurants and coffeehouses. The street was still avoided by old-time residents of the neighborhood, but newer res-

Potomac Street, 1992. *A false-alarm brought fire trucks, fire fighters, and neighborhood gawkers to the street in this photo taken from the roof of 51 Potomac Street. (Author's Collection)*

idents viewed it with less jaundiced eyes and increasingly patronized the new businesses.

I recorded the following observations of Haight Street in May 1986:

> Haight Street has changed dramatically in recent months. Six new restaurants and a variety of small shops have opened. Most are operated by young people and cater to the Punk-like crowd of youth that dominates the street. Several galleries offer art to a variety of tastes. Small fashion shops cater to the sometimes bizarre styles of today's youth – as do hair salons where one can have hair cut and dyed in ways unimaginable. It would appear that we have become the "punk" center of the city. It is an entertainment to merely watch the parade of outrageous costumes, make-up, and hair-styles pass on the sidewalks. These trendy places will probably be followed by more mainstream businesses. A few have already come, such as a new fish/meat market at the corner of Haight and Fillmore where the Bank of America used to be. A Thai restaurant is doing very well at the corner of Waller and Fillmore, a space once occupied by a dingy pool hall. It seems only a matter of time before our little stretch of Haight Street joins the "respectable" neighborhoods of the city.[42]

A feature story in *Calendar Magazine* the following year concurred with my observations:

> The Lower Haight is in the middle of a transition that makes it unique in the city. Its streets are peopled by individuals who might not meet anywhere else: blacks, the long-time residents of the neighborhood, gays attracted by the proximity of the Castro, young professionals looking to buy a house cheap and fix it up, and hip folk attracted to the plethora of bars, cafes, restaurants and off-beat stores. All make room for each other on the sidewalks, occasionally even stopping to talk.[43]

Except for tree-planting in the mid-1980s, Potomac Street changed little visually. All houses had been painted and sometimes renovated during the previous decade. Blacks continued to leave the street. Young White couples purchased homes on the street, had children, and then as the children approached school age, sold their homes and moved to the suburbs or a more desirable part of the city – usually having realized a considerable profit on the sale of their properties. Only one White family remained on the street as their children attended private schools located some distance from the neighborhood.

By 1983, the number of African American households on Potomac Street had declined significantly. Only thirteen of them remained while White households had grown to twenty-three. The Filipino American households remained constant at four. The ethnicity of other households included Japanese-American as well as mixes of African American/White, African American/Latino American, White/Chinese American, and White/Latino American. The compositions of these households included nine nuclear families, six widows, five lesbian couples, five gay couples, four childless married couples, two extended families, and one group of unmarried straights. The composition of six households was unreported.

Probably the most memorable event of the 1980s for most Potomac Street residents was the earthquake of 1989. Although damage on the street was minor compared to other parts of the city, residents nonetheless experienced broken windows, damaged foundations, cracked plaster, and toppled chimneys. Immediately following the quake, people fled their homes for the open safety of the street and park. Most remained outdoors for hours, swapping quake stories with neighbors as they listened to news reports on portable radios and nervously watched smoke fill the skies above the badly damaged Marina District. Some of the more skittish remained in the park all night, fearful that aftershocks would bring additional destruction to their homes and injury to themselves.

During the 1990s, more Whites moved to Potomac Street and the Lower Haight. Haight Street continued to attract the young counterculture set. Many lived in the area but others came from throughout the city and the Bay Area to patronize the restaurants, clubs, bars, coffeehouses, tattoo parlors, and body-piercing salons that catered to their tastes. The street still had a heavy influx of African Americans from the nearby projects, and despite occasional violent encounters, they evolved a somewhat harmonious, albeit tenuous, relationship with the newcomers.

In 1993, the San Francisco Housing Authority announced that the crime-ridden, deteriorated public housing projects on the 300 block of Haight Street would be demolished and replaced with townhouses for low income residents.

In 1994, the *San Francisco Chronicle* once again described the Lower Haight:

> Near the other end of the [Lower Haight] strip, a brace of Generation X slacker types – baseball caps cranked aft – are nursing espressos at the sidewalk tables of the Horse Shoe coffeehouse. But two blocks away, it's crack, not caffeine, that is the drug of choice at the hulking projects that squat at the corner of Haight and Buchanan. . . .

It's the young who seem to dominate street life. On a recent warm afternoon, the Lower Haight was flush with youthful gawkers, café loungers and latter-day boulevardiers. They are denizens with attitudes, black Army boots, nose rings and hair that often comes in primary colors. Their politics are summed up by six bumper stickers pasted to the front door of a two-story walk-up; Rats Have Rights Too, Keep Abortion Legal, Pro Life My Ass, Food Not Bombs, No War, and Meat Stinks.

And they help support a surprisingly large commercial district including 18 restaurants, 16 retail merchandise and clothing shops, nine bars, nine storefronts whose business mission is unclear, eight service operations including tattoo removal and bookkeeping, seven coffeehouses, seven markets, six barbershops and hair salons, four record shops, three art galleries, three laundries, three liquor stores and one drugstore.

Many of the businesses have an underground, alternative bent. Others are just bent.[44]

By late 1994, the number of African American households on Potomac Street had dropped to only five and three of these were widows living alone. White households had grown to twenty-eight. Filipino Americans remained constant at four and two households were African American/ White mixes. The composition of the households was very diverse and reflected the larger surrounding neighborhood: six nuclear families, five widows, five gay couples, four straight women roommates, three straight men and women roommates, three unmarried straight couples, and three lesbian couples. Others were a brother and sister and their roommate, a brother and sister, a childless married couple, a straight man, a widow and her son, a divorced woman and her adult daughter, a gay man, an extended family, two straight men, three gay men, and a mix of gays and straights. The population of the street was only 100, the lowest since it was established.

The escalation of real estate prices continued. The 1989 earthquake slowed prices somewhat, but they soon began soaring again. Single family homes that sold for $50,000 in 1976 were selling for a million dollars by the turn of the century. In the late 1960s and early 70s, abandoned buildings of flats sometimes sold for back taxes, but they would sell for millions when converted to condominiums or tenants-in-common during the following decades. Increasingly, poor households were forced from the neighborhood by the high rents that accompanied the rising real estate prices. The newcomers were almost all White and during the 1990s, the neighborhood

changed from a predominantly African American neighborhood to a predominantly White neighborhood.

In 1996, the crime-ridden projects in the 300 block of Haight Street
were demolished and new townhouses were built for low-income families. More careful screening of new tenants as well as closer monitoring of
drug and criminal activities resulted in reduced crime and violence for the
neighborhood. This public housing complex became the last concentration
of African Americans in the Lower Haight.

The Haight Street turnaround continued. Increasingly, the commercial
corridor catered to the newcomers with an explosion of coffeehouses, bars,
hair salons, trendy clothing shops, and restaurants.

2001–2007

In the early years of the new century, Potomac Street underwent several infrastructure projects which included the installation of new sewer,
gas, and water lines. The most visible change resulted from the removal
of the unsightly tangles of overhead electrical wires on the street. In 1997,
Potomac Streeters joined residents on the parallel block of Pierce Street
and the two intersecting blocks of Waller Street and petitioned Pacific Gas
and Electric Company to underground the electric wires and install new
street lamps. The undergrounding began in 2002, but was not completed
until February 2005 when the old poles were finally removed. After the
infrastructure projects were completed, the embattled street was repaved.

Haight Street attracted increasingly mainstream businesses in the early
2000s. A plethora of restaurants currently dominates the street that feature
cuisines from around the world including India, Thailand, Japan, Pakistan,
Mexico, El Salvador, Iraq, Ethiopia, and Jordan as well as such standard
American fare as pizza parlors, hamburger joints, sandwich shops, and
coffeehouses. Bars, clubs, boutiques, and hair salons satisfy other needs of
the neighborhood. The artsy-youthful counterculture still flavors the street,
but it is relinquishing territory to stroller-pushing mothers, recovering
dot-commers, jogging computer-geeks, and ageing baby-boomers. The
public housing projects in the 300 block of Haight Street are still predominantly African American, but the current residents increasingly participate
in the larger neighborhood.

Occasional murders, muggings, and break-ins in the Lower Haight
reminded residents as well as outsiders that some of the violence of years
past was still in the neighborhood. One of the tragic incidents for Potomac
Street residents was the murder of Raymon Bass who was shot and killed

in the 400 block of Haight Street in May 2004. This popular teenager who lived with his great-grandmother at 64 Potomac had recently graduated from high school and planned to attend university on a football scholarship.[45] Such tragedy was not new to the household: three other members of the family were killed over the years, a personal reminder to Potomac Street residents of the tragic lives of many inner-city African Americans.

As the neighborhood changed, so did Duboce Park. Many neighborhood meetings of the late 1990s and early 2000s were dominated by the conflict between dog-owners and non-dog-owners (especially parents) over rights to the park and whether the park should be designated off-leash for dogs. An uneasy compromise was eventually reached with canines assigned to the lower park and people to the upper park. In 2001, a new playground in the park illustrated the increasing number of families with small children in the vicinity. A neighborhood drive to fund construction of a labyrinth in the park along Scott Street was finalized with the dedication of the structure in 2007. At the time of this writing (December 2007), Duboce Park is once again undergoing renovation. The Harvey Milk Recreation Center is being retrofitted and remodeled while redesign of the lower park features new sidewalks to demarcate the dog portion of the park. Several of these projects have unfortunately further diminished the park's green space.

Resurfacing Potomac Street, 2006. *After repeated excavations for new sewer, water, and electrical lines, Potomac Street received a new surface in 2006. (Author's Collection)*

Across the park, California Pacific Medical Center – née German Hospital, née Franklin Hospital, and née Ralph K. Davies Medical Center – is undergoing yet another transformation. More buildings are being crammed into the hospital block as the complex is modernized and enlarged to meet its perceived contemporary needs.

In November 2007, only eighty-seven people lived on Potomac Street, the smallest population ever recorded for the street. Three factors are responsible for this reduced population: the greater affluence of the current residents, the smaller sizes of families, and five vacant units at the time of the census. In former years, residents in both flats and houses rented rooms to lodgers to generate additional income. Today these units are inhabited by affluent individuals, couples and families who can afford the spaces without renting to lodgers. The current families on Potomac Street are considerably smaller than the families of earlier years. The largest family today has three children while most have only one child. When the five vacant units on the street are occupied, the population will probably increase by ten for a total of ninety-seven, still the lowest figure in the history of the street.

Today the households of Potomac Street are predominantly White: twenty-two are White, three are Filipino American, three are African American, two are White/African American, two are White/Latino American, three are White/Chinese American, and one is White/Iranian American.

In 2007, diversity continued to characterize the household composition of Potomac Street. These households included seven nuclear families, four straight married couples, four straight unmarried couples, three gay couples, straight unmarried couples sharing a household, four gay men living alone, two straight women, two straight women and a straight man, two widows and child/children, two straight men, one straight woman, three straight women, one lesbian, a gay couple and a straight woman, and a straight male with his son, daughter-in-law, and roommate.

A significant recent change in the neighborhood is the large number of former rental units that are passing into owner-occupancy. Some have been converted to condominiums but others have sold as tenants-in-common whereby several people purchase a multiple unit building and each owns and resides in a unit. Seven former rental units on Potomac Street have been converted to condominiums and six others are in the process of becoming tenants-in-common.

This change in tenancy is altering the character of the Lower Haight. Renters tend to be young, racially diverse, and childless whereas home-owners are older, White, and frequently have children. The youthful, multi-racial dynamism that characterized the Lower Haight for many years is being

Renovation of Duboce Park, 2007. *The park was again renovated in 2007 to demarcate a dog-exercise area in the lower end. A sidewalk across the lower park to Duboce Avenue, eliminated in the 1979 renovation, was reinstated. (Author's Collection)*

replaced by an older, more conservative White population. Ironically, the colorful vibrant neighborhood that initially attracted the newcomers is being subdued by their very presence. Some call it "the suburbanization of the city" and suggest that the newcomers are bringing their suburban values to the city and thereby creating a suburban-like culture in the urban setting.

But whatever the subculture that emerges from the present cauldron of the Lower Haight, the history of Potomac Street reveals one certainty: That subculture will eventually be altered and perhaps absorbed by the inevitable next wave of change that arrives in the neighborhood.

Summary

Population. As illustrated in Table 1, the population of Potomac Street has varied over the years. When the first Potomac Street census was conducted in 1900, only six houses were occupied and the population was twenty-five. By the 1910 census, all but one of the current houses on the street were occupied for a total population of 149. In 1920, the population was unchanged. Although the 1930 census is incomplete, it suggests that the population had not changed much since 1920. The 1940 census reports 125 residents for Potomac Street. No other population figures are available for the street until 1994 and 2007. The street probably remained at its 1940 population until World War II. During the war, many people moved to San Francisco and housing became critical as dwellings were subdivided

44

to accommodate the influx of newcomers. Several Potomac Street flats were subdivided into smaller units at this time, and many private homes rented out rooms. The street probably reached its highest population during the war years, although there is no way of knowing what that figure may have been. By 1994, the population of the street had dropped to 100 and in 2007, it was only eighty-seven. Part of this decline resulted from the conversion of several buildings on the street from apartments back to their original flats during the 1970s, but probably most important was the greater affluence of the residents. The large flats on the street were once occupied by individuals, couples or small families who supplemented their incomes by subletting rooms to lodgers. In more recent years, the flats have been occupied by childless couples or two or three roommates. Increasingly, fewer children lived on the street. In 1994, nine children lived on the street, the lowest child-population in the history of the street, and in 2007 that population remained constant.

Table 1
Population of Potomac Street

	1900	1910	1920	1930	1940	1994	2007
Adults	14	125	119	92	105	91	78
Children	11	24	30	17	20	9	9
Total	25	149	149	109	125	100	87

Nativity. In 1900, over half of Potomac Street's adult population was foreign-born (see Table 2). By 1910, when the street was fully occupied, a third of that population was foreign-born. In 1920, the foreign-born residents dropped to one-quarter. The incomplete 1930 census also reports one-quarter of the residents were foreign-born. All these foreign-born people were from Europe, most from northern Europe. Approximately the same percentage was foreign born in 1940. No other figures are available until 1994 when only ten percent of the population was foreign-born. That percentage remained the same in 2007. The early figures probably reflect figures for the city at large since the late 19th and early 20th centuries were periods of heavy immigration into the United States. The 1994 figures, however, do not reflect San Francisco's population at that time which was thirty-four percent foreign-born. Nor does the 2007 Potomac Street population of foreign-born residents reflect the large immigrant population of the city.

Table 2
Nativity of Potomac Street Adults

	1900	1910	1920	1930	1940	1994	2007
U.S.	6	84	89	68	89	81	79
Foreign	8	41	30	24	36	10	8
Total	14	125	119	92	125	91	87

Ethnicity. Since its beginning, Potomac Street has been an ethnically diverse street, but the composition of that diversity has changed over the years (see Table 3). The censuses of 1900, 1910, 1920, 1930, and 1940 identify all residents of the street as "white" – except for one resident who identified as a Spaniard in 1930. Beneath that homogeneity, however, was a great deal of ethnic diversity, albeit within a northern European context. For example, in 1910, a third of the adult population was foreign-born and represented such countries as England, Ireland, Sweden, Canada, Germany, Scotland, Russia, and Australia. By 1920 that number had dropped to one-quarter. The incomplete 1930 census also reported one-quarter of the population as foreign born, the vast majority from northern Europe. No figures are available again until 1994, but it is likely that ethnicity did not change much on the street until World War II, although the number of foreign-born probably continued to decline. In the late 1940s and early 1950s, the first non-White residents moved to the street, namely Filipino Americans and African Americans. Until the early 1960s, the street remained a mixture of Filipino Americans, African Americans, and Whites. African Americans dominated the street throughout the late 1960s and most of the 1970s, until Whites began to return. In 1994, the street was predominantly White with four Filipino American households, five African American households, and one mixed White/African American household. The street lacked members of two large ethnic groups found elsewhere in San Francisco, namely Chinese and Latinos. Over the years, a few Chinese and Latinos lived on the street but their numbers were never large. The 1994 White population was much more homogenous than in earlier years; only two were foreign-born. In 2007, the ethnic mix had not changed greatly. If the five units that were vacant at the time of the 2007 census had been occupied, the number of White households would probably approximate the 1994 number.

Table 3
Ethnicity of Potomac Street Households

	1900	1910	1920	1930	1940	1972	1980	1986	1994	2007
White	6	31	37	30	42	11	21	25	28	22
African American						24	9	11	5	3
Filipino American						4	4	4	4	3
Japanese American						1	1	1	1	
African American & White						1	3	3	2	2
Chinese American & White							1	1		3
Latino American & White										2
Iranian American & White										1
Total	6	31	37	30	42	41	39	45	40	36

Household Composition. Quantitative data for household composition is lacking for Potomac Street between 1940 (the last available U.S. census) and 1972 (see Table 4). In 1910, the first census after the completion of house-construction on Potomac Street, only nine nuclear families lived on the street. By 1920, that number had grown to sixteen. The incomplete 1930 census reported ten nuclear families. In 1940, there were thirteen such families. No figures are available again until 1972, but most likely the earlier numbers prevailed until the changes of World War II. Probably the 1950s and 1960s had many nuclear family households, albeit of different ethnicities from earlier ones. The later decades saw a decline in nuclear families as childless couples (married and unmarried), unmarried individuals, and gay and lesbian couples moved to the street. Accompanying this change was a decline in the child population. Extended family households were more numerous in earlier censuses, but they have always been few. A significant change occurred in the number of people, especially widows, who lived alone. In the official U.S. censuses, no household was occupied by only one person: such persons (unmarried individuals, widows, and widowers) lodged or boarded with other households. In the 1970s, 1980s, and early 1990s, these single people occupied their own households or, in the case of some young unmarried adults, they rented a unit and lived together as a group.

Table 4
Household Composition of Potomac Street

	1900	1910	1920	1930	1940	1972	1983	1994	2007
Nuclear family	3	7	16	10	13	6	9	6	7
Nuclear family & boarder	1	2	2	2					
Nuclear family & servant			1						
Nuclear family & parent				2					
Married couple	1	6	5		8	6	4	2	4
Married couple & parent				2					
Married couple & boarder	1	2	3		3	1			
Two unrelated married couples		2	1						
Two unrelated unmarried couples									1
Unmarried couple								3	4
Gay couple						4	5	5	3
Lesbian couple							5	3	
Lesbian									1
Single parent family		5	2	4	2				
Single parent family & boarder			3						
Father, son, daughter-in-law & boarder								1	
Extended family		5	6			2	2	2	
Extended family & boarder			1						
Widow						4	6	5	
Widow & child/children									2
Widow & boarders		2	1		1				
Unmarried man					2				2
Unmarried man & boarders				1	3				
Unmarried men						4	2	2	
Unmarried woman					4				1
Unmarried women						1		3	2
Unmarried men & women						3	3		2
Gay men								1	1
Gay & straight								1	1
Brother & sister				2				1	
Brother, sister & roommate							1		
Gay man						1		1	4
Unknown						6	6	3	
Unoccupied units						3	2	1	5
Total	6	31	41	23	36	41	45	40	40

East side of Potomac Street, 2003. (Author's Collection)

Occupations. The changing occupations of Potomac Street residents reflect other changes on the street. The 1900 census reveals that the small population was equally divided between white-collar and blue-collar workers (see Table 5). By 1910, when all houses on the street were occupied, white-collar workers outnumbered blue-collar workers. White-collar workers had grown somewhat larger by 1920. The incomplete 1930 census reported almost an equal number of white- and blue-collar workers. The 1940 Census reveals a preponderance of blue-collar workers on the street. The figures for 1944 are based on voter registration and therefore incomplete, but they nonetheless probably reflect the larger population. After 1944, occupations are not provided on the voter registration reports. I have no figures for the 1970s and 1980s when I lived on the street, but blue-collar workers definitely predominated during those years. The numbers for 1994 reveal that the occupations of Potomac Street were once again predominantly white-collar jobs. In 2007, the vast majority (forty-six) of the street's work force were white-collar workers with only four blue-collar workers. Seven retired blue-collar workers also lived on the street at that time.

Table 5
Occupations of Potomac Residents

	1900	1910	1920	1930	1940	1944	1994	2007
White-collar	3	36	41	23	20	32	57	48
Blue-collar	3	14	26	21	38	27	27	4
Total	6	50	67	44	58	59	84	52

Political Affiliation. The changing political affiliations of the people on Potomac Street reflect the trends of San Francisco in general (see Table 6). The voter registers for 1912, 1920, and 1930 reveal a predominance of Republicans on the street with Democrats a weak second. By 1940, the situation was reversed with Democrats far outnumbering Republicans. In 1950, Democrats were still in the lead. No voter registers are available for the 1960s, 1970s, or 1980s, but in 1994, Democrats still led Republicans who were an even smaller minority. The 1994 list reveals a greater number of smaller parties, such as the Green Party and the Peace and Freedom Party, illustrating the liberal politics of San Francisco. I have no figures for 2007, the year of this writing, but the street is currently predominantly Democrat.

Table 6
Political Affiliation of Potomac Street Residents

	1912	1920	1930	1940	1950	1994
Republicans	53	44	36	21	18	7
Democrats	13	11	12	66	57	63
Other*	2	14	3	4	3	24
Total	68	69	51	91	78	94

Potomac Street is over one-hundred years old. Its history is a microcosm of the surrounding neighborhood and in some ways of San Francisco itself. Indeed, its changing, dynamic history is somewhat typical of American urban history.

If the original residents of Potomac Street returned to their little street, they would find many of the old buildings still intact, but they would discover a very different neighborhood. Today, the Lower Haight reflects the larger San Francisco population of Blacks, Whites, Asians, Latinos, Middle Easterners, lesbians, gays, straights, young, and old. And for those of us who live on Potomac Street, that mix of people is our very special home as well as one of the most vibrant neighborhoods in the city of San Francisco.

---

* "Other" includes those who declined to name a party, those who claimed no party affiliation, and those who named specific parties other than Democrat or Republican.

PART TWO

MUSINGS AND MEMORIES

1972–2007

47-49-51 Potomac Street, 1984. Marc Scruggs and I moved into this late Victorian building on Potomac Street overlooking Duboce Park in 1972. Many of the observations recorded on the following pages were made from the upper windows. (Author's Collection)

Introduction

I MOVED INTO the late-Victorian building at 47-49-51 Potomac Street overlooking Duboce Park on 15 October 1972. Marc Scruggs and I were looking for a flat large enough for two gay men to share comfortably. After several days of searching in the Mission, Western Addition, and Upper Haight – and encountering more than one landlord who obviously didn't care for the shade of Marc's skin – a color-blind property-owner directed us to a vacant flat in his three-unit building on Potomac Street that bordered Duboce Park in the Lower Haight. He warned us that the flat was a mess, recently vacated by leftover flower-children of the Haight-Ashbury era.

We followed his directions and found Duboce Park. The park was disappointing, filled with broken glass, dead grass, trash, and dog feces. Hostile-looking Black children played on broken-down play equipment and two old men, one Black and one White, sat on fractured benches sipping from brown paper bags. A few trees fronted unpainted houses that lined the north side of the almost-treeless park.

The house we were seeking was the most imposing (as well as the most dilapidated) building on the park. Its three stories were filled with bay windows overlooking the park and its multi-colored patched roof hosted two dormers and a turret. It was once gray, but that was long ago and now the paint was peeling to the boards. The bottom and top floors appeared occupied, but the second floor was obviously empty. Curtainless windows stared blankly at the derelict park.

But even in its disrepair, the house attracted us. It looked like an aged duchess who had fallen on bad times and could no longer afford the wardrobe her station warranted. It seemed to ask us to come inside. We crossed the park to Potomac Street where the entrance to the house was located. Although the owner had warned us the flat was in bad shape, we were not quite prepared for the broken-down furniture, abandoned clothes, dog feces, and garbage that cluttered the place. We later learned that the former tenants who left the mess were a street theater group called The Angels of Light, an off-shoot of the legendary Cockettes, a counterculture music group of drag queens and hippies spawned during the late-1960s flower-child era of Haight-Ashbury. Housekeeping was not their forte.

After the initial shock, however, we were able to see through the smell and debris to the bright airiness of the flat. After viewing dozens of flats with bay windows at the front and the back with much gloom and darkness in between, we were impressed with the abundant light that flooded the rooms. It lacked the heavy, sometimes oppressive Victorian decor, but rather was quietly understated. We discussed how the flat could be made into a beautiful home if enough work and money were invested. We decided, however, that we didn't want to take on the chore so we returned the keys and told the owner we would look elsewhere.

We went home to my studio apartment and thought about the flat. The next day we decided to check out the Duboce Park neighborhood again. We walked around and talked to people to get a feel for the area. After much thought on our part and many encouraging calls from the owner, we decided to rent the flat for $260 a month with a monthly $25 rebate for the painting and cleaning we would invest to make it livable.

We painted and cleaned for two weeks, and moved into the flat at 49 Potomac Street in mid-October 1972. By Christmas we had finished the renovation and settled down to enjoy our new home. Two years later in 1974, we bought the building and moved upstairs to 51 Potomac Street. Shortly after we moved in, I began a journal of my observations of Potomac Street and Duboce Park. The following is an edited version of that journal.

West side of Potomac Street, 2007. (Author's Collection)

THE JOURNAL

3 November 1972

This poor derelict park! Patches of dead grass, an ancient palm tree with one tired frond, broken wine and beer bottles scattered on the sidewalks, garbage overflowing from unattended trashcans occasionally set afire by children, broken-down play equipment, winos on dilapidated benches, the occasional hooker or dope-pusher from Haight Street openly peddling, and dog shit everywhere. No wonder some people call it "Dog Shit Park."

What a lovely little park it *could* be.

16 December 1972

Potomac Street is a sad-looking little street. Most of the late-Victorian facades of its houses are intact except the house directly in front of us which has one of the ugliest remodeling jobs I've seen in the city. Virtually every house needs a coat of paint. The street is usually clogged with cars overflowing onto the sidewalks. Periodically someone abandons a mattress, a sofa, a tire, a water heater, or bags of garbage on the sidewalks. Despite the nearby park, the neighborhood kids usually play in the street, reluctantly moving aside as cars come and go. Dope dealers routinely meet in front of our house and hand out parcels to distributors who magically emerge from the park and then disappear with their elixirs. A flat across the street rents rooms by the hour to hookers and their tricks from Haight Street. Resident hookers in a ground-level flat at the end of the block solicit passers-by from their windows. Police cars come and go day and night, but never seem to do much.

When we leave the flat, we always walk across the park and avoid Potomac Street and the no-man's land beyond. Why did we move here? I frequently ask myself that question.

1 February 1973

Two elderly sisters visit the park daily. They live mid-block on Walter Street. Each always wears something red – a stocking cap, a scarf, a coat, or gloves. Thus, we call them the "Red Sisters." Every morning they deposit their garbage in one of the park trashcans. Then they visit the restaurants of upper Market Street, entering separately, never buying anything but surreptitiously pocketing packets of sugar and jelly, napkins, and toilet paper. Each day they visit different restaurants and because they take only a few items, the merchants tolerate them. One died recently, but the other continues her rounds, always dressed in red.

24 April 1973

Yesterday when I was in the dining room, I happened to glance out the window and saw a cluster of Black children in the center of the park curiously encircling two young White men. Upon closer examination, I discovered that the young men had three very long snakes, apparently pets they were exercising in the park. After about fifteen minutes of slithering here and there, the snakes coiled around their owners who then carried them homeward down Noe Street.

5 April 1974

> *In the dark night,*
> *a faraway foghorn laments its lonely plight.*

15 May 1974

An older Black man, probably in his mid-60s, was a frequent visitor to the park when we first moved here. He was genial to all as he walked his little white dog. He developed an amorous relationship with a White woman over on Walter Street and began spending more and more time with her, much to his wife's chagrin. One night during sex with his mistress (so we were told), he died of a heart attack. His irate wife refused to claim his body or have anything to do with his funeral. I occasionally see her walking the little white dog in the park looking none too happy about anything.

16 August 1975

I've come to expect the bizarre in Duboce Park, but occasionally I am still surprised – like last week. We were eating dinner in the dining room. About midway through our meal, a White woman entered the park from Duboce Avenue. As she walked toward our house, she began slowly removing her clothes and tossing them aside. When completely disrobed, she threw her arms back and began singing "Jesus Christ, Superstar." By this time about a dozen children were gathered around her, squealing and giggling. She finished her song, turned to a startled young White man walking his dog nearby and embraced him in a great bear hug. Meanwhile, an elderly Black woman passing through the park picked up the discarded clothes and wrapped her own coat around the nude woman. Then, she and the young man gently led her out of the park.

We never saw the woman again. Perhaps she was high on drugs or simply high on life. How shocked the Victorian builders of this house would have been had they witnessed the scene. But for us it was just another incident – not exactly routine, but not exactly extraordinary either in this city that San Francisco has become.

12 November 1975

Each evening, a father brings his crippled son to the park. The boy, about ten, wears heavy leg-braces and must be carried piggyback by his father from their home on Duboce Avenue. They play catch and other games that demand little leg movement. Then the father patiently instructs his son in a series of leg exercises. After a half-hour or so, the father hoists his son onto his back and carries him home. A lot of love flows between that father and his son.

5 February 1976

Early this morning at the first hints of dawn, the park was covered with a light blanket of snow. The air held a strange sort of hush as if a ghost from another land had crept in and no one knew quite how to deal with him. But soon the early rays of day devoured the whiteness of the city and left only Twin Peaks wearing a wintry mantle.

I wonder how many times Duboce Park has hosted snow.

22 February 1976

As I watch the park today, I muse that the founders of the park would be happy to see what I see. They might not approve of some of the skin-colors beneath my window and they would certainly disapprove of some of the clothing, but they definitely would approve of the way such a mosaic of people is enjoying this little park called Duboce.

Central to the park activities is a group of young White men – bearded, long-haired, and countercultured – playing the establishment game of volleyball in the triangle of green in front of our house. Beneath me a young couple is refinishing two chairs as they enjoy the warm sunshine. On the upper greenery, a large Black man patiently teaches youngsters the rudiments of baseball, preparatory to the coming season. Three colorful kites overhead announce it is once again that season of the year. A half-dozen people lay in the grass soaking up the fresh warmth of spring sunshine.

Children of various ages, sizes, and colors skillfully race down the sidewalks on multi-colored skateboards. A couple of Black winos, one blind and one quite seeing, exchange stories as they watch the activities and sip ephemeral happiness from brown paper bags. Two girls on newly acquired roller skates grip the cyclone fence as they cautiously wheel their way down the sidewalk along Duboce Avenue. Children swing in the swings while two tiny tots experience the marvel of sand through fingers. Dog-owners, using their animals as vehicles for communication, stop to chat about matters doggy and otherwise. The old green streetcars add their comfortable clatter to the gentle park sounds as they appear and disappear at the tunnel. And all is drenched in sparkling sunshine from a crackling blue sky, studded with puffs of white clouds.

A day so perfectly beautiful that somehow it hurts a little bit.

27 June 1976

Today Duboce Park hosted an unplanned celebration. The Gay Pride Parade was scheduled to terminate at Duboce and Noe where awaiting Muni busses would transport participants to Golden Gate Park. The planners underestimated the crowd, however, and hundreds of people flooded into the park faster than busses could carry them away. Bare-breasted women and jock-strapped men were among the more conservatively dressed revelers. A parade float pulled into the lower end of the park, blasting loud rock music, and for about three hours the park jumped with celebration. A few skirmishes broke out but for the most part it was a joyous occasion until the float departed and a group of neighborhood toughs threw beer bottles in unfond farewell.

The park was a shambles when the crowd dispersed, littered with bottles, cans, papers, and other debris. Patches of grass already suffering ninety degree temperatures from the previous week were stomped into the bare earth. Marc and I helped other neighbors pick up the mess that was left behind. Hopefully, more planning will go into the event next year.

28 June 1976

Today a large extended Black family of about forty members is barbecuing in the park. Several of them live on Potomac Street. A table is loaded with food, and chairs are set-up for the elders. The younger adults are in charge of barbecuing the chicken and ribs while children scurry about in their rough-and-tumble games. A radio provides music and lots of laughter punctuates the gathering. Everyone is in great spirits obviously enjoying one another's company as they invite passersby to join the party.

When most outsiders view this neighborhood, they see a crime-ridden Black ghetto, failing to see the strong families, churches, businesses, and community organizations that provide basic human needs to its residents. Today they should witness the warmth and love and joy of the family in the park and perhaps they would better appreciate the human dimensions of the neighborhood.

4 December 1976

> *White sea gulls*
>> *on green grass*
>>> *beneath a gray sky.*
>>>> *San Francisco winter.*

6 February 1977

One could write a book about the people of the park, the little-known denizens who come and go each day.

An old Filipino man who lives on Duboce Avenue brings the small children of his extended family to play in the playground each morning while he sits back and paternally observes.

A little old Armenian woman – ex-dancer, ex-gambler, ex-twin, ex-God-knows-what-else – walks her pack of twenty-four dogs individually, in pairs, and in threesomes throughout the day.

An elderly Chinese woman greets each morning with Tai-chi.

A boxed-out boxer shadow-boxes in the park for hours and hours and hours.

An autistic Black child builds towers with stray park stones and sifts sand through long sensitive fingers, experiencing a world I will never know.

An old painter in his beret and goatee enjoys retirement with his old dog and a fuller dedication to his art.

An angry Scandinavian man, portly and fearful, walks his aggressive muzzled dogs, carrying a claw-hammer to battle real and imaginary foes.

A blind Black man with a white cane sits on his regular bench, offering the world a drink as it passes by.

And all the others who come and go – kooky, quaint, sane, and sometimes crazy. The denizens of Duboce Park.

25 February 1977

> *How healing is a beautiful morning.*

13 March 1977

Many of the changes in the neighborhood in recent years stem from an influx of middle class Whites into a low income Black neighborhood. Property prices have sky-rocketed and real estate speculators are rampant. One of the last eyesores and chronic problem areas is the 500 block of Haight Street. Three bars continue to attract large numbers of hustlers, dope-pushers, pimps, prostitutes, derelicts, and just plain people. Sometimes several hundred of them mill along the north side of that block. Several real estate speculators with property in the block have tried to close the bars by legal means to no avail. Last Thursday, we heard that some of the disgruntled owners planned to burn the buildings to get rid of the bars and the Blacks they attract. This morning at two a.m. we were awakened by the sound of fire engines. From our upstairs window, we could see the sky above Haight Street ablaze. We walked over and, unsurprisingly, the backs of the bars in the 500 block of Haight Street were burning. As I watched the flames, a seasoned Black hooker standing alone beside me cried softly to herself: "Why do they hate us so much?" Probably the final knell of an era – and the beginning of White respectability ushered in on the wings of violence, hate, and amorality.

3 May 1977

Outside my window,
a tree
turbulent in the evening wind.

31 May 1977

We are in the midst of a drought which has been adequately chronicled elsewhere. Suffice it to say, the park has suffered. I've never seen it so dry. Patches of earth appear throughout the yellow grass. The maintenance crew grudgingly releases a few ritual drops of water each day, teasing the thirsty grass. The past two winters have been too, too dry. I yearn for an old fashioned wet winter. Maybe next year.

1 June 1977

Some nights the yesterdays seem so long ago
and at other times, only a blink away.

21 August 1977

I was enjoying a late afternoon cup of tea in the front window overlooking the park when suddenly a very naked young man with a mane of red hair appeared seemingly from nowhere, obviously high on something. He wandered through the park, stopping occasionally to roll in the grass, indifferent to the stares of people. He stumbled to the play area and tried to cover himself with sand until some children on bicycles frightened him and chased him out of the park. When I last saw him, he was running down Duboce Avenue, long red hair flowing and appendages bouncing.

Another Sunday afternoon in Duboce Park.

23 August 1977

Tonight, a thick fog transforms Duboce Park into an island surrounded by muffled grayness. The faces of the Duboce Avenue houses stare at me, their roofs and chimneys invisible in the fog. It is a very private world with only an occasional intruding streetcar reminding me of another reality beyond the fog.

17 December 1977

The rains have finally come and like healing hands embrace the thirsty land. This morning the park is a great green emerald, domed by a gray sky and punctuated by a lone white seagull meandering its way through the damp grass.

A wet, thankful San Francisco greets the morn.

11 March 1978

Two recent events may signal a new era for Haight Street. A restaurant called "Daddy's" opened in the 400 block and next to the infamous Hank's 500 Club (now closed but once synonymous with dope, hookers, racketeering, and murder) a flower shop opened. These are the first new businesses on the street for some time. Residential buildings have been renovated throughout the neighborhood, but the commercial blocks of Haight Street are still rundown and filled with hundreds of people in the evenings and night – some kinky and criminal, but most just plain folks socializing with their friends.

10 August 1978

The fog excludes me from the world.
Or excludes the world from me?

1 February 1979

We have been away from the city for several months. We followed the Jonestown tragedy and the assassination of George Moscone and Harvey

Milk in newspapers while traveling in Europe. It seemed unreal from that distance, but the city is still recovering from the all-too-reality of the tragic events.

7 February 1979

Few children play in the park anymore. Black kids once filled the park and I miss them. I miss their games, their youthful energy, and the happy sounds of their play. Fewer and fewer Blacks are in the park as the neighborhood changes.

The renovation of houses continues and the neighborhood is no longer an urban blight. Haight Street lags, but even much of it is sporting a new coat of paint. Small businesses come and go, but most commercial buildings are unable to attract the kinds of businesses they want. The street crowd persists, albeit greatly diminished from its earlier days, a mere fraction of the hundreds that formerly congregated there. It is obviously only a matter of time before the transformation from a low income, largely Black neighborhood to a middle income, largely White neighborhood is accomplished.

The last house on our street has been painted. Since we painted our house in June 1974, every house on Potomac Street has been painted and several have changed ownership. What a transformation in five short years.

13 February 1979

Sea gulls regularly visit the park in winter when storms drive them from their seaside homes. Their arrival is always a treat and today over a hundred of them dot the green grass beneath my window. Occasionally they are frightened and a flurry of white passes my windows, circles and then lands again. Their whiteness enhances the brilliant green grass which reminds me of young rice fields in Bali.

28 February 1979

For several days, a boy has brought his puppy to play in the park. It is delightful to watch them. They race together, the chubby little pup puffing after the boy. Then they stop, roll in the grass and hug. They warm the chilly day.

1 April 1979

For some months now, the city has been testing the new streetcars late at night when traffic has thinned. The cars are orange and white, super-sleek, and probably much more comfortable than the old green ones.

But I am sad to see the old ones go. They always remind me of friendly, green caterpillars wiggling their way up and down Duboce Avenue. I enjoy their bright lights and comfortable clatter. The new ones seem less intimate, less friendly.

7 June 1979

Finally, the renovation of Duboce Park is happening. After almost two years of planning and waiting, workers arrived on Monday to begin work. The dilapidated play equipment has been dismantled and workers with deafening jackhammers are removing the concrete walkways. The ugly cyclone fence along Duboce Avenue is gone. A large earth-moving machine scraped off the top soil in high areas to fill in low spaces. The park is now a grassless, barren field hosting occasional dust swirls whipped up by the wandering wind. Children enjoy the piles of dirt and clods more than they ever enjoyed the old playground. Dogs are baffled by the loss of their familiar sniffing spots. Several men with Geiger counters wander the grounds in search of Indian-head pennies, old horseshoes, ceramic shards, and other treasures.

The houses around the park observe it all with boredom, as if they saw it happen before and it made little difference to them. They're a bit dusty, but otherwise unchanged by all the activity in their front lawns.

14 June 1979

The poor park looks like a disaster area. For over a week now, bulldozers have chewed away at it. The little hills are gone, as well as the pathways, the playground, and the shrubbery. Only a few large trees remain. The air is filled with dust and the heavy equipment shakes our house like a minor earthquake. Only an empty, barren scar of earth remains – and if you listen closely, you can almost hear the old park weep.

20 June 1979

This morning the park is filled with trailers, trucks, and portable dressing rooms. Scenes for a film called "Die Laughing" are being shot in some of the abandoned buildings on Waller Street. Much excitement for neighborhood denizens.

25 July 1979

I have learned from several sources that the park was a dumping ground for rocks when Duboce Avenue was cut through the hill where the United States Mint now stands. The current excavation in the park certainly confirms that. Beneath a foot or so of top soil are serpentine rocks which were apparently dumped over the entire park. Some of the same rocks were used for the foundation of our building. When the park was first established the bigger rocks were piled and planted in rock gardens.

14 September 1979

Last night Marc and I were returning home from North Beach at midnight and noticed several police cars at the corner of Steiner and Waller. We stopped to investigate and learned that a man had been shot by two other men who fled down Steiner Street and into the park. This morning as we walked up Steiner, we followed a very visible trail of blood to Haight Street. A grim reminder that some of the neighborhood's lurid past is still with us.

18 September 1979

A disturbing event to record. As we left the house tonight, we heard shouting and whistles. A young Black man came running up the park, pursued by a group of the holier-than-thou Holy Order of Mans blowing whistles and shouting that the young man had stolen something. He picked up a rock to ward them off and ran down Potomac Street with the pack of White whistle-blowers in hot pursuit. It seemed a not-too-subtle symbol of how Blacks are being pushed from this neighborhood by Whites. And perhaps equally symbolic was the horde of Christians chasing the frantic young man like a pack of hounds after a fox. It was terribly distasteful and disturbingly like a lynch mob.

I'm not sure I can handle the White middle class respectability that is creeping into the neighborhood.

3 October 1979

A Black father beats his small son in the park. Doesn't he know the unkind world will give his son many beatings? Now he needs his father's love so he can survive those future beatings.

16 November 1979

The park is almost finished. The rains have come and the newly planted grass is brilliant green. Almost a hundred trees have been planted. After the brown scar of summer months, the greenery is healing. New streetcar tracks are almost completed on Duboce Avenue. Hopefully before long all construction will end and a degree of normalcy returns to the neighborhood.

16 December 1979

Today we held holiday open house for our neighbors on Potomac Street. We served holiday punch, eggnog, cookies and cheeses. Many guests brought additional food and drink. It was pleasant to chat with people I knew from only brief encounters on the street. Our little street has evolved into quite an amiable neighborhood with a pleasant mix of ages, races, and genders.

27 December 1979

A tragedy in our neighborhood. On Christmas Eve, Mrs. Marjorie Smith (whose husband owns the building next to us) left for church at 10 p.m. to attend late services. When she did not return home at the expected time, her family became alarmed and began searching for her. She was eventually found dead in her car, shot in the head. I think of her husband and children and the terrible grief they are experiencing this Christmas.*

31 December 1979

New Year's Eve.
A full moon and foghorns
conclude another decade.
And the houses on Duboce Avenue
stare their blank stares,
indifferent to new years.

15 March 1980

One of spring's delights on Potomac Street is the blooming of the plum tree at the park-end of the street. Laden with white blossoms, it is startling in its whiteness. People stop to smell its blossoms and marvel at its beauty. In early summer, we will once again have a bumper crop of plums – if the neighborhood kids don't pick all the green ones to pellet one another.

29 April 1980

Last Saturday the newly renovated Duboce Park was dedicated, sponsored by yet another neighborhood association – this one called "Friends of Duboce Park."

It was a successful event. A portable stage, sponsored by the city, was erected at the Steiner Street end of the park. Mayor Dianne Feinstein

---

*A poem about this tragedy written by Tanya Joyce, a longtime resident of Potomac Street, appears in Appendix Six.

and other city dignitaries appeared with a few appropriate political words. Music groups performed throughout the day and a bake sale was sponsored by the park association. A teepee was erected on the new hill in the park where a storyteller entertained children.

The ethnic composition of the neighborhood continues to change. When we first moved here, almost all the children who played in the park were Black. Now we see a sprinkling of Whites and Asians. The same is true of adults. More and more young Whites are finding the neighborhood an attractive, convenient place to live. No small attraction is the new N-Judah line which speeds people under Market Street to downtown in half the time. The neighborhood is a far cry from the neighborhood we moved to eight years ago.

30 April 1980

Of the many strange denizens of the park, one is particularly peculiar. We call her "dog-woman." She has four dogs that she regularly brings to the park and lets them shit wherever they wish. Periodically she comes to the park to perform penance. With a small shovel and can, she dances through the park, searching for dog turds. When she spots one, her eyes light up and she triumphantly swoops upon it and deposits it in her can. When the can is full, she empties it into a trashcan and dances back in search of more prey. She performs an important job in the park, but my, what a strange soul.

10 May 1980

During the past year, muggings and assaults in the neighborhood have increased. Several have been Black teenagers attacking young Whites, some gay but not all. I witnessed one tonight from the dining room window. A young man was waiting at the streetcar stop as six young Blacks walking up Duboce Avenue approached him. One crossed over to speak to him, and then suddenly all six jumped him. By the time I reached the stop, the assailants were gone. Needless to say, such attacks do not improve race relations.

18 August 1980

At dawn
a scarlet sun incarnadined the world.

27 December 1980

Potomac Street observed its second annual Christmas party. Last year we hosted an open house for the street, but this year, the Johnks at

44 Potomac hosted the event. It was a great success. An eighty-four year-old neighbor had a grand time. So grand, in fact, that she called a friend the following day to enquire how she got home. She awakened in her bed the next morning with no recollection of having arrived there and was afraid she had drunk too much and "disgraced herself." The neighbor assured her that she was escorted home by the host and her behavior was strictly above board.

4 January 1981

The commercial corridor of Haight Street is slowly making a comeback. Most of the street people are gone and many newly renovated stores are ready to rent. But the reputation of the street lingers and businesses are still reluctant to come in. A produce store, a coffeehouse, a record store, a wine and cheese shop, a restaurant, and a taqueria are all recent arrivals. However, about twenty-five storefronts still remain blank and waiting. Perhaps this will be their year to host new businesses.

12 January 1981

The awful hours of sleeplessness.

16 March 1981

A refugee Hmong family suns in the park. The mother and baby wear remnants of their native dress. The others wear odds and ends of Western clothes. They are the newest ethnic group in the neighborhood. What pain, cruelty, and death have brought them to Duboce Park from the hills of Southeast Asia? Despite their smiles, suffering never completely abandons their faces. And probably never will.

23 May 1981

Hmong children now play in the park. They initially walked shyly through the park with their parents, wearing odd combinations of ethnic and American clothes. Increasingly their clothing became Americanized and increasingly they visited the park without their parents. Today, dressed entirely in American garb, they play soccer indistinguishable from other Asian-American children. How rapid is the Americanization process – at least on the surface.

3 November 1981

A tragedy on the street. A young Latina woman who lived in the basement flat at 54 Potomac Street shot herself last night. A word or a small act might have saved her life, but no one knew. A chill to an otherwise beautiful November day.

18 November 1981

Frequently, I'm amazed at what perfect fools people make of themselves over their dogs. Seemingly normal people lose rationality and social graces when they tangle over their canines. They spout insults and foul language at one another they would never use in other contexts.

Dogs sometimes attract a particular type of closet-fool.

28 April 1982

Each morning four Chinese elders stroll slowly through the park. I can set my watch by their arrival. At nine, they enter from Steiner Street. The man leads the way. He walks a few steps, hands held behind him, and stops to inspect the grass and small flowers. Behind him are three women, usually in single file. Sometimes they talk, but most often they do not. They have probably spent their entire lives together and no longer have much to say to one another. They sit on the benches for a half-hour or so, observing park activities. Then they depart in single file led by the old man. Tomorrow they will return at nine o'clock.

2 May 1982

How quickly the green hills of winter
become the golden hills of summer.

23 May 1982

Our little park has become a haven for sunbathers. The warm days bring them out in droves: this morning I counted fifty basking in the sun. It is a White crowd for the most part, Blacks probably secretly thinking it a rather ridiculous ritual.

A fire on the street last week. The top floor of 74 Potomac caught fire. Extensive damage was limited to the front rooms, but smoke and water damage spread throughout the unit. Anyone who lives in a Victorian house fears fire. It is so devastating to these old wooden buildings.

25 May 1982

Watching the children go to school is one of my morning entertainments. Some go reluctantly, seeking distractions along the way as they trudge through the park. Others stop for games of catch, hopscotch, or jump rope. Still others race through the park with uncontained exuberance, eagerly anticipating another day at school. But some seem to resent each step that takes them closer to the classroom.

Today little Zeb is not looking forward to school. His head is down forlornly as he sucks his thumb, pulls an oversized lunchbox, and drags unwilling feet over the sidewalk. This will not be an easy day for him.

We sometimes forget the painful days of childhood.

26 May 1982

An elderly woman lived in the middle of the block for many years. An African American, she was very fair and passed as White most of her life. When we first moved here, she still got out and about, usually dressed to the nines.

One day I saw her dressed in bright blue, complete with matching purse and hat, headed for the streetcar stop. When I asked her where she was going she replied that she heard the COYOTE convention of prostitutes was meeting downtown and she was going to check it out since she had known such women in her youth.

Although into her 80s, she still had a strong libido. Once when I visited her, I noticed a stack of pornographic magazines beside her bed. Two men in the neighborhood told me she invited them to her home on lame pretenses, and then tried to seduce them.

She once admitted that she supplanted her pension by faking falls on Muni or in downtown stores and then agreed to out-of-court settlements. She was always a bit cantankerous, but over the years she became increasingly senile and alienated most people on the street in one way or another. She called the police frequently, usually claiming someone had committed murder or was trying to kill her. A recurring claim was that someone had killed babies and buried them in a basement or backyard.

She eventually sold her home and moved to a nursing home, but periodically she hired a cab and returned to her house insisting the new owners were occupying it illegally.

One of Potomac Street's colorful characters.

23 February 1983

Spring has arrived at Duboce Park. The acacias and flowering plums are in bloom. Less conspicuous are the tiny wild flowers tucked away in the grass, gems of beauty for those who seek them out.

4 March 1983

Dogs!

  Dogs!

   Dogs!

    Romping hilariously in the park!

30 March 1983

Potomac Street is getting trees. Several years ago, we planted trees in front of our building at 47-49-51 Potomac as well as the one we own at 71-73-75 Potomac. We hoped neighbors would follow our lead and now it has happened. Recently the neighbor across the street gathered contributions from people on the street for trees and this Saturday, volunteers will plant them. Their greenery should soften our little street considerably.

3 June 1983

According to a neighbor who has lived at 569 Duboce for over sixty years, three service stations were once at the end of the park – one on the northeast corner of Steiner and Hermann, one on the northeast corner of Duboce and Steiner, and one on the southeast corner of Duboce and Sanchez. The first site remains as an auto repair shop, the second is an empty lot, and the third is a public housing complex for the elderly.

12 December 1983

We have a new sign in the park. Recently a handsome sign on a green pole was erected near the streetcar stop announcing to the world that this is indeed Duboce Park.

27 January 1984

A bit of a tizzy in the neighborhood. The church across the park rents out its facilities to various religious congregations. One such congregation is a downhome-style Black group who like their religion loud and long. Their raucous enthusiasm has caused some neighbors to complain, but so far their services are still rocking the neighborhood.

3 March 1984

Occasionally I see someone in the park enjoying a moment of sheer contentment. This morning a young Black man sits in the grass among the small flowers on the hill, cuddling his puppy in the warm sunshine. Sometimes it is a small child who discovers a flower or perhaps an abandoned ball with a smile of utter happiness. Or maybe it's an elderly person sitting on a bench soaking up warm sunshine with a warm smile on a warm face. It's a moment when everything is perfect, nothing could improve the present. The next moment may demand a return to the mundane business of survival, but for this moment all is right with the world.

One could do worse than sit in the warm sunshine in Duboce Park on a beautiful spring morning.

23 March 1984

The elderly Chinese group that comes to the park with such regularity at nine in the morning is down to three now. The old man is not with them anymore. He probably misses his morning walks and the tiny surprises he found along the way. Perhaps he is dead now. I miss him.

4 June 1984

A sleepless night
listening to the mating calls of foghorns.

7 July 1984

One could write a history of Duboce Park based on the characters who make the park their home for a few days or weeks and then move on. Since we have lived here, numerous characters have dominated the park – if not dominated, at least were the most noticeable presence. In the early years, it was two winos, a Black one and a White one who held court each day on the benches. A deranged young man came along later and spent his days shadow-boxing in the park. Later a pacer walked back and forth across the park all day long and into the night. Recently a man claiming to be the "sheriff" of Duboce Park periodically stalks the park searching for who-knows-what. Presently, a Black woman and a White man come to the park each day and await the birth of their child.

Probably such people have always sought the park, and probably they always will.

27 September 1984

Some new businesses in the Haight-Fillmore area have opened – a coffeehouse, a frozen yogurt shop, and a crêpe restaurant. The long-awaited Walgreen drugstore at the Haight-Fillmore intersection will open soon.

23 October 1984

One of my entertainments is watching people react to their dogs' defecation.

Some are very concerned, watch closely as their animals go through evacuation gymnastics, and then examine the results carefully, checking texture and color. Such concerned people usually pick-up. May they be blessed in heaven.

Others are embarrassed by the whole procedure. They look away, pretending interest elsewhere, and then furtively swoop up the turds when the dog is finished, hoping no one has seen them. They, too, deserve a place up there.

Others slowly walk away when their dogs begin squatting, pretend they have seen nothing and, of course, do not pick-up. Dante's hell has a special circle for them.

Some drive up in cars, let their dogs out to do their jobs, then call them back and drive away. They, too, have a special circle reserved in Dante's inferno.

And then there are the civic-minded souls who arrive at the park with shovel and bag in hand, merrily scooping up each and every dog turd they spot. They will receive their special reward in heaven!

11 December 1984

Just when I think I've seen all there is to see of the unexpected in the park, I see more.

This afternoon I was working in my study and happened to glance into the park. Under a yellow blanket in the middle of the park was a great deal of activity. Closer watching revealed arms, legs, heads, and buttocks in the unmistakable movements of fornication! It was a young couple making love in the middle of the park. Passing people and sniffing dogs gave them no concern. They finished, adjusted their clothes, picked up their blanket, and walked away arm-in-arm.

What next? I don't know, but I suspect this, too, will be topped.

27 December 1984

Another death to report. Betty Dilley lived on the street for thirty years in 67 Potomac. She died recently after suffering a debilitating stroke about a year ago. She was a plucky little White woman who stuck with the street during its toughest days.

Now I suppose her house will be sold.

24 May 1985

A cool, gray day. Too many days without sunshine. Not my kind of weather. Another death on the street: a young man in 75 Potomac died,

the first AIDS death on the street. The fear of the dreadful disease is growing in the city. This will surely be recorded as one of the darker chapters
in the city's history. The death rate is now in excess of one a day and most
San Franciscans have been personally touched by the disease. The rest of
the world does not yet understand the AIDS crisis as we do here in San
Francisco.

1 June 1985

A pleasant interlude in the park. Marc was working in front of the
house and called me to watch some bees swarm. The building at the end of
the park on Steiner Street keeps bee hives on its roof. One of the hives split
and swarmed in the park as a crowd gathered to watch. The bees flew in a
tornado-like cloud and alighted on an unsuspecting shrub. A bee-keeper
appeared, donned in appropriate garb, and managed to coax the bees into a
hive and carted them away. A small reminder that we and the dogs are not
the only creatures that inhabit this park.

Much tree planting in the neighborhood in recent months on Waller,
Steiner, Germania, Hermann, and Fillmore. Several hundred trees have
been planted with city funds and efforts from the neighborhood coordi-
nated through Friends of the Urban Forest. As they reach maturity, the
neighborhood should be transformed in yet another way.

This is not the neighborhood it was when we moved here thirteen years
ago. Almost all the vacant lots are filled with new houses and most derelict buildings have been renovated. Ethnic composition has shifted from
a mostly Black neighborhood to an increasingly White one. The presence
of the projects on Haight Street slows further change, but when they are
renovated, even more dramatic changes will occur.

3 June 1985

White filaments of clouds
flung across a blue sky
beyond my window.

6 October 1985

Two boys and their dog play ball in the park. One boy pitches, the
other bats, and the dog retrieves. A very efficient trio!

23 October 1985

The AIDS epidemic has come closer to home. The new roommate of the two men in the flat below has AIDS. The dreadful disease continues unabated.

Good news. The unsightly auto-repair business (formerly a filling station) at the corner of Steiner and Duboce has been sold and residential units will be constructed on the site. The same contractor who built the tiny houses on Steiner at Germania and Hermann bought the land and will fill the lot with more tiny houses. The project should considerably enhance the neighborhood.

Dan White committed suicide. He did, it seems, what he wanted others to do. A flood of sad memories for San Franciscans.

26 October 1985

Since the 1930s, a bar has occupied the ground floor of the second building on the west side of Sanchez Street near Duboce. I once heard it was an Irish pub for many years. When we arrived here in 1972, it was a lesbian bar called "Scott's Pit," later it became simply "The Pit." It was always a rather tough place and toughened more over the years when it began attracting the motorcycle crowd. Adding to the mix was a loony old man across the street whose favorite pastime was hurling insults at the patrons as they arrived and departed. Finally, neighborhood pressure and a poor bar manager were the death knell for The Pit. Now the entire building is undergoing extensive renovation. If the walls of that old bar could talk, the workmen would be shocked. Some tough characters frequented that place in its heyday.

14 November 1985

Sad news this week. We learned that the man who sold us this house, Joseph Gross, died of heart failure. We lived here for two years as his tenants and then bought the building from him. José (as most people called him) was a colorful character, a bright man who seemed to know a little bit about everything. He was a collector and his properties were crammed with things he was unable to relinquish. I shall miss José. He was a rare edition, and such are increasingly hard to come by.

29 November 1985

A film called "The Times of Harvey Milk" won an Academy Award as best documentary last year. It was based on the life of Harvey Milk, concentrating on his political career in San Francisco as the first openly gay supervisor. A scene in the film was set in Duboce Park and this house dominates the background. Another modest claim to fame for the old house.

17 December 1985

Last Sunday, the three young men who rent the middle flat hosted an open house to celebrate Christmas and collect food for needy AIDS patients. It was a great success with several hundred people in attendance.

20 December 1985

Savoring tea in the library
in the warmth of winter sun.

21 April 1986

A tragedy while we were away. A young man who lived in the flat below died of AIDS four days after his diagnosis. Ten people within my social circle have died of the terrible disease.

21 May 1986

Millions of tiny, white flowers carpet the green park today.

23 May 1986

A restless night
terminated by the first streetcar.

18 November 1986

I see only two of the elderly Chinese women from the little group that used to visit the park. They are very crippled now. Probably I will not see them much longer.

3 December 1986

Three houses on Potomac Street were houses of "ill repute" when we moved here. Directly across the street, a woman named Stella lived in the middle flat. She was an older Black woman, always high on something, who rented rooms by the hour to hookers from Haight Street. Day and night, they arrived with their tricks, yelling up to Stella for a key. Money was openly exchanged and the couple disappeared upstairs, returning a few minutes later. The front apartment at 73 Potomac was occupied by two White women who catered to a mixed clientele. They were raided several times by the police. When we bought the building in 1977, we discovered a note scrawled on the back of a bedroom door: "Best fuck I ever had!

This place has my recommendation!" The lower flat in the building at the southeast corner of Waller and Potomac was occupied by an assortment of male and female hookers. It was an active place and also had its share of police raids.

As I recall those early years, I understand why our friends thought we were insane to buy in this neighborhood.

25 April 1987

The AIDS epidemic continues. The rest of the nation and the world are now gripped in the fear that we experienced in San Francisco several years ago.

One of our favorite neighbors moved while we were away this past winter. A Black woman, Sylvia Brown, lived in the middle front apartment next to us on Potomac Street since the 1950s. She moved to a retirement home in the Western Addition. She was a kind soul with a marvelous laugh that spread joy to everyone within hearing. We shall miss her. Each year we lose another old friend from the street. It is not the warm, friendly little street of a few years ago when everyone knew one another.

28 April 1987

Since the trees have become established, we have more birds in the park. Two industrious finches are building a nest beneath our dining room windows.

Several daycare centers have opened in the neighborhood. Each day small herds of children are brought to the park playground. Some seem too tiny to be separated from their mothers.

29 April 1987

Over the years, the park has occasionally served as rehearsal space for musicians with questionable talents. They were probably driven from their digs by roommates, spouses, and neighbors who couldn't tolerate their sounds. So they sought the park to harass those of us who live along it. For years, bongo and other drums were beaten mercilessly beneath our windows. Occasional flutes, clarinets and trumpets added their misplaced notes. For several weeks, a tired saxophonist contributed his mournful plight to the cacophony. This morning, a guitarist on the bench below has strummed the same monotonous melody for two hours. May his fingers soon lock in place.

4 May 1987

The world will never miss a grain of sand,
Nor a person living without love.

15 May 1987

So many homeless people in the park these days. Each morning they emerge from sleeping places among the trees and shrubs.

21 May 1987

Two deaths on the street this week. Mr. Ransom Collins, an elderly Black man who lived in the bottom flat next door, died after deteriorating health. He was in his mid-80s and his death was hardly unexpected, but nonetheless I am saddened. He was a dear man, always with a quiet smile and good word for everyone. Another elderly Black man, Mr. Crenshaw, also died. He and his wife lived in the top flat above the grocery store at the corner of Potomac and Waller. They owned the building and for many years Mrs. Crenshaw and her sister operated the small grocery store called "Two Sisters" on the ground floor. They sold delicious barbecued chickens as well as cigarettes by the "stick." I suppose they will be replaced by the ever-increasing mainstream Whites who are moving into the neighborhood.

One of the recent projects of the Holier-than-thou Order of Mans is ridding the park of the homeless people who sometimes sleep here. They call the police who harass them until they move on. Their special brand of Christian charity.

Finally, the little houses are materializing on the former service station lot at the corner of Duboce and Steiner. They are certainly tiny. I think all ten of them would fit into the first floor of our flat.

24 May 1987

Today was the celebration of the 50th anniversary of the Golden Gate Bridge. This evening's celebration included fireworks. We climbed to the top of our roof and had a ringside (albeit somewhat chilly) view of a spectacular display of colorful explosions.

21 June 1987

The second look-alike house uphill on Duboce Avenue caught fire last week in the early morning. Marc saw the blaze, phoned the fire department, and we crossed the park to see if we could help. The garage and first story burned badly, but the rest of the house suffered only smoke and water damage. The owner has been renovating the house for several years and finally finished it a few months ago. He was, of course, devastated.

22 June 1987

Again the police have come to chase the homeless people from the park. Their only crime is they have no place to go. Others sunbathe in the park all day, but the homeless are not allowed a small space for more than a few hours.

2 September 1987

Happy birds fill the park with songs.

5 October 1987

We are in the grip of a heat wave with temperatures over 100 degrees. The entire city is gasping as long-closed windows are pried open to catch a breeze that refuses to blow. People wander aimlessly through the park in the alien stifling heat, or sit on front steps sipping relief from cool aluminum cans. As the night deepens, they reluctantly return to stuffy homes hoping tomorrow will usher fog through the Golden Gate.

10 October 1987

I now see only one woman from the elderly group of Chinese who regularly visited the park in the mornings. She walks slowly, hands behind her back, looking at the ground. She sits on a bench for awhile, watching park activity, and then departs. Probably all her companions are dead now. She seems so lonely, a relic from another era.

2 November 1987

The tiny houses at the corner of Duboce and Steiner are almost finished. Ten are squeezed into that small space. They have turned out rather well and blend nicely into the surrounding architecture. All the formerly empty lots around the park are now filled.

2 December 1987

In the extra stillness of a still, still night,
I sometimes hear the centuries whisper on a silver slice of moonlight.

24 April 1988

An awful mural commemorating Harvey Milk has been painted in garish colors on the south wall of the recreation building. Fortunately, we cannot see it from our flat.

5 May 1988

A neighborhood character died last week. "Carol Murphy" was one of the many aliases she used. I haven't the foggiest idea what her real name was – she had so many. In her late 70s at the time of her death, she lived on 14th Street across from Davies Hospital.

We met Carol when we painted our house for the first time in 1974. She walked two small dogs in the park and stopped to chat with us as we worked. We learned that she lived with about two dozen dogs and an old Filipino man who helped her with the animals. When we met her, she was having trouble with city inspectors who wanted to inspect her building. She didn't want them in her flat because of the dogs and the deteriorated condition of her building. She did everything she could to elude them. She pretended she was mute if they arrived when she couldn't hide in time. If they knew she was inside, she pretended she was Chinese and made sounds she thought were Chinese. At the time we met her, the inspectors had given her a deadline for an inspection and were threatening to come with the police if she did not comply. We decided to help her. So we rented a van, put all the dogs in it, and parked it down the street. While she and Marc kept the dogs quiet, I took the inspectors through the house. What an excursion that was! Her flat was crammed with clothes and household items she had collected over the years. Paths led from room to room. The clutter was so great the inspectors lost their way several times and could not determine the number of rooms in the flat.

Carol was a character. Her parents were Armenian immigrants who came here after the great slaughter in Turkey. She was raised in Sacramento and with a twin sister began running away to San Francisco at an early age. The two sisters finally moved to the city and during the 1930s, they were a popular dancing nightclub act. Carol drove Packards and Cadillacs, and proudly drove the third car across the Bay Bridge when it opened in 1936.

Last week, Carol suffered a stroke and lay in her home alone for two days before a neighbor heard her pounding on the floor for help. She was taken to a hospital where she died.

The city has lost one of its colorful characters. Many, many stories could be written about Carol or Victoria or Darlene and all her other aliases.

6 May 1988

A neighbor told me about a strange exhibitionist who lives in the top apartment on the northwest corner of Steiner and Waller. Each morning at one o'clock, he strips and masturbates in his brightly lighted bay window to assembled voyeurs below.

Just when I thought the neighborhood was improving.

15 May 1988

In the event that a future resident of 51 Potomac Street should remove the wallpaper from the bedroom with the curved exterior wall, I should mention that beneath that painted wallpaper is a mural. It is painted mostly in green tones in the psychedelic art style of San Francisco's Hippy era of the late 1960s. We saw it when we were tenants in 49 Potomac before the then-tenants of 51 wallpapered over it. A neighbor informed us that the young man who created the mural eventually moved to New York where he became a successful Broadway set designer. So future resident: If you remove the wallpaper, do so gingerly for you might uncover a modern masterpiece. Maybe.

1 April 1989

I have just returned home from visiting a friend at Davies Hospital who is dying of AIDS. Bill is a very talented composer who still has much to give the world. How many young men with AIDS have died in that hospital that towers over our little park? How many have spent their final hours looking at this spot of green? And how many more will there be? Will there be a worse chapter in the city's history than these dark days of AIDS? Surely not.

6 April 1989

Bill died last night.

15 May 1989

> *Homeless people in the park*
> *— so much time to kill before death.*

15 June 1989

Our house has been painted again. The same colors – a white body with sashes of dark green, the original colors of the house. We replaced the old redwood rain gutters with copper ones. We reluctantly gave up the old ones, but they were in bad shape. We are also repairing the front stairs balustrades and newel posts. We painted the building twice ourselves, but this time is for someone else. All of the work cost about $14,000. It seems a small fortune to me. Will some future reader think it was a bargain? Probably.

16 October 1989

This evening a group of about 150 people marched down Sanchez Street and arrived at the park for a rally protesting U.S. aid to the El Salvador government. Flood lights illuminated the central park as various speakers spoke. After about an hour of speeches, the group dispersed. This is the first large gathering I have seen in the park in some time.

18 October 1989

Yesterday at 5:04 p.m., the Bay Area experienced its worst earthquake in recent years. I was in the shower when it struck. I left the shower and stood in the bathroom doorway, clinging to the door to keep from falling. I saw bookcases falling in my study across the hall and heard crashes throughout the flat. It seemed the entire building was collapsing. I have no idea how long the quake lasted. It seemed forever. When it finally stopped I quickly dressed and Marc and I explored the flat. My study was a shambles with fallen bookcases and books strewn everywhere. We ventured down to the main floor. The worst havoc was in the library where toppled bookcases spewed books throughout the room and knocked over chairs, plants, and lamps.

We expected major structural damage to the building, but thankfully none is evident. Some walls have serious cracks and two windows were broken.

We joined the throngs of people in the street and park where several hundred congregated in small groups. Electricity was out so we relied on gossip and transistor radios to learn about the damage throughout the city. We heard about the collapse of the Bay Bridge and the freeway in Oakland. Fire engines and police cars sounded sirens throughout the city. To the north we saw black clouds of smoke from the fires in the Marina District. We remained on the front steps late into the night talking with neighbors and passers-by. When we finally went indoors, small groups of people remained throughout the park, huddled around lamps. Some slept in the park, fearful of aftershocks that might bring additional havoc.

This evening a group of people gathered in the park to sing and celebrate their survival of the earthquake.

19 October 1989

The other day I was in the dining room and happened to glance into the park. Beneath my window, a street person was lying under a blanket in the unmistakable final stages of masturbation. He finished, wiped himself and moved on. The public nature of his masturbation did not disturb me so much as did the sad realization that he had no private space for performing that very personal act.

21 October 1989

People continue to cleanup after the quake. Broken windows, toppled chimneys, and plaster damage seem the extent of most damage in the neighborhood although a few buildings suffered serious structural damage. Reports of the devastation of the quake elsewhere continue and we increasingly realize how fortunate we were to suffer so little damage.

10 November 1989

We are still experiencing quake aftershocks but life is slowly returning to normal. Next week the Bay Bridge is scheduled to reopen. The only good news emerging from the quake is that some of the ugly freeways in the city were damaged and will be demolished.

29 November 1989

Haight Street continues to evolve. When we first moved here it was mostly bars, boarded up storefronts, junk shops, and the occasional mom-and-pop store specializing in cheap wines. We now have a drugstore, a meat and fish market, a used bookstore, a produce store, and a grocery store. In addition several specialty shops cater to the growing off-beat youthful White population. Two night clubs specialize in live jazz, and four coffee-houses accommodate local caffeine needs. Restaurants feature cuisines from India, Mexico, Italy, China, Japan, Vietnam, and Thailand. We regularly dine on Haight Street now whereas in years past we never ventured there. In the evenings, a lively street market peddles a variety of goods displayed on the sidewalks. A sense of creative energy and enthusiasm pervades the street as the Haight-Fillmore neighborhood is rapidly becoming the Greenwich Village of San Francisco.

"Posties" (post-yuppie, post-hippie, and post-punk) is what the press has labeled the new breed of young people on Haight Street. The *Chronicle* proclaims the Haight-Fillmore as the new in-place. It is filled with young people seemingly in competition to see who can dress the most outrageously. Who will follow the Posties?

6 December 1989

A heavy fog arrived last night,
cozied up to our windows
and left the world dripping.

3 April 1990

We are having a beautiful spring. The park trees are in glorious bloom – the pinks of the plums, the yellows of the acacias, and the fresh greens of the sycamores. Birds sing to establish mating territory and people drop here and there in the grass to soak up warm sunshine. The sort of spring day poets write about.

9 May 1990

A handsome young man dressed immaculately in a dark business suit sits on a park bench devouring a sandwich so hungrily that he belies his affluent appearance.

28 May 1990

TV crews once again descended on our park. The house directly uphill on the park from us has been used several times to film scenes for the popular TV program "Midnight Caller," a suspense drama set in San Francisco. The second house uphill was used for scenes in the TV mystery series "Murder, She Wrote." The neighborhood was all astir as celebrities and crews took over the area for a few hours.

29 May 1990

Puppies in the park. A smiling crowd gathers to pet and cuddle them. We need more puppies in the world.

28 November 1990

I'm up early this morning. A night mist has dampened the thirsty park. The eastern hills lighten an awakening park. In the distance, a single, straight column of smoke rises above the pinkening hills while two lone birds cross the empty sky. A few yellow leaves stubbornly cling to the bare sycamores outside my window. A man in a bathrobe sleepily walks an energetic little dog. Streetcars, too brightly lighted for the early morning, emerge from the tunnel with a few sleepy passengers. A distant airplane slowly and quietly climbs into the sky. One by one, streetlights switch-off. A jogger darts across the park, adding too much speed to the early morning. Birds seek breakfast in the grass. A garbage truck arrives with too much noise. Suddenly a brilliant sun explodes over the hills and floods the world with light. Another day for Duboce Park.

1 December 1990

In recent weeks, activist gay groups have held nighttime rallies in the park for more government spending on AIDS. Loud and long with bright lights.

AIDS still grips the city.

24 January 1991

That certain slant of afternoon winter sun.

29 April 1991

Another death on the street. The mother of Mrs. Trammell who lives at 64 Potomac died last week. She arrived here from Oklahoma about five years ago to live with her daughter. When asked why she came to San Francisco, she quipped, "I came out here to find a man." She was 107 when she died and still sharp as a tack, an African-American woman who lived through an important century of her people's history. What an archive of experiences died with her.

20 July 1991

A homeless man in the park.
Like a fly, he will die
Unremembered.

30 September 1991

Yesterday two men came to blows over their dogs in the park. One kicked the other's dog. The other slugged him. Shouting and vulgar threats followed. The assaulted one left the park and returned with policemen in search of the assailant, but he was nowhere to be found. Dogs are occasionally stuck with strange owners.

11 October 1991

The strange man who dresses his two dogs in blue jeans and plaid shirts adorned one with a mask, eye glasses, and wig today. Such indignities some dogs must endure.

20 October 1991

A terrible tragedy today. Fire started in the Oakland Hills this morning and quickly spread out of control. Many homes have burned and many people displaced. Dark clouds of smoke hover over the city, turning a sunny day into twilight. Tonight we can see flames across the bay as the fire still burns out of control.

1 December 1991

A woman on the street who has lived here since the 1950s has become an alcoholic over the years. It is so sad to see her decay. Every day, she leaves her home to buy a bottle, visiting different stores so she will not appear too regular at any one of them. She has become obese and has trouble managing her stairs as she goes in and out of her house. She lives alone and recently installed bars on her doors and windows. Such terrible demons she must battle in the empty, lonely horror of her home.

25 December 1991

Two birds perched on bare branches.
One, large and brown.
One, small and white.
Unlikely companions on a Christmas morning.

14 May 1992

The headlines of recent days are the riots following the Rodney King beating verdict. Last Friday night a demonstration began in Dolores Park and marched toward Duboce Park. The police broke up the demonstrators and arrested some 300 participants as they approached our park. Many people, much noise, and dozens of policemen filled the neighborhood. Much controversy currently fills the newspapers about the legality of the arrests.

17 May 1992

The park is hosting an event today. Protestors of the arrests made last Friday at the aborted march protesting the Rodney King trial have called for a demonstration which will begin in Duboce Park and march to the Civic Center. So far about a hundred people have gathered, mostly young and White. Various banners with political slogans are scattered around the park. A stage for speakers is erected near Steiner Street and portable toilets are on Duboce Avenue. Musicians are playing and singing protest music. Speakers denounced the Republican administrations of recent years and the inequities of the economic system. The speeches were indistinguishable from one another, sophomoric radical ritual that never seems to accomplish much. Unfortunately, the injustices will go on.

After the speeches, the group dispersed and marched up Steiner to Haight toward the Civic Center.

29 May 1992

I wonder how many generations of youth have come to this park, sat in the grass to reflect on the nature of the world, and arrived at the same conclusions. The world has changed greatly, but I wonder if youth and their questions have changed. Probably not much. Strip them of their current garb and jargon, and I suspect they are indistinguishable from the youth who first visited this park almost a hundred years ago.

11 June 1992

Unable to sleep at four a.m., I gaze into the park. So quiet and empty. Scattered lights reveal fellow insomniacs. A prowling cab stalks the streets. A young man emerges from Walter Street and crosses to Potomac – perhaps someone's late trick. Another man, tall with flowing blond hair, walks up Duboce Avenue with a bag of groceries from Safeway. A homeless man sleeps on the bench at the streetcar stop. Ominous white clouds populate the dark sky. A strangely quiet time. A private time.

13 June 1992

Many nights I see a ragged, old Black man walk up Duboce Avenue to the streetcar stop where he sleeps on the bench. He is a big man, covered in layers of filthy rags. I have seen him on the street and sensed the loneliness in his face. He has no one to touch him, talk to him, or hold him. Many such souls wander the sidewalks these days. Some are homeless street people, but many are the mainstream denizens of the city. Alone in urban isolation.

6 December 1992

A death on the street. A young divorced woman who lived with her small child at 68 Potomac died of cancer. She was a Christian Scientist and refused medical treatment. I did not know her.

25 December 1992

A quiet night.
Christmas night.
A cold, dark night.
The park's emptiest night of the year.
Only the homeless and the restless walk the streets.
An old man wrapped in rags wanders through the park.
I wonder what Christmas means to him.
Probably nothing.
As with me.

31 December 1992

The old year ends with rains in the Bay Area and blizzards in the Sierras. The long drought is over and a sense of euphoria pervades the city. How good it is to have an old-time San Francisco winter. I hear no complaints about the wet, cold weather. The end of the drought and a new president – not a bad way to begin a new year.

Happy New Year.

8 April 1993

A gregarious dog in the park
  – startled that birds are unreceptive to his friendliness.

28 April 1993

Another death in the neighborhood, a young man named Leander who lived on Germania Street. An early casualty of drugs, he was pursued by many personal demons. Some days he was fine, but other days he ranted down the streets, half-dressed and screaming at the world. AIDS eventually claimed him. Your terrible pain has ended, Leander.

2 May 1993

Excitement in the park. A young man was sunbathing in the nude. Someone was offended and called the police. By the time they got here, he had packed up and gone home.

28 May 1993

The man in the bottom flat died today – or I should say his body was found today. He probably died last night. His sister came to visit him this morning and after receiving no response from the doorbell, she asked us to let her in. She and Marc found his body in the dining room, sitting in the chair where he had been watching television. His life was not a happy one. He was alienated from almost everyone, including his wife, family, and neighbors. He died alone as he had lived his final years while cancer ate away at his life. Probably few will miss him, the ultimate fate of all of us.

I wonder how many people have died in this house.

27 November 1993

Last night a fire consumed several buildings at Haight Street and Pierce. About two a.m., I was awakened by fire engines that would not stop screaming. I looked out the sun room windows and saw flames leaping into the sky on Haight Street. I awakened Marc and we walked over. Fire engines were still arriving and before long the corner building and six others were ablaze. It was terrifying to see the fire burn out of control, leaping from building to building, a reminder of how vulnerable these old wood buildings are. Neighborhood rumor claims the fire resulted from an explosion in an illegal drug lab. One man died in the conflagration.

The neighborhood lost several beautiful Victorian buildings last night.

1 December 1993

The olive trees along Duboce Avenue have bumper crops of fruit this year. Several people have harvested the ripe olives. I hope they know what to do with them – fresh from the tree they are inedible.

Occasionally I see a civic-minded soul whose efforts I applaud. He periodically wanders the neighborhood sidewalks with a paint brush and a bucket of paint and paints out the graffiti on posts and walls. Needless to say, he has a full-time job.

16 December 1993

A shooting at the end of Potomac Street a few weeks ago. Members of a household on the street opened a flower/gift shop at the corner of Potomac and Waller. It attracted a hanger-on crowd of rather tough Black youth. The other day one shot at another. He missed, several police cars arrived and brought much excitement to the street. I haven't heard the outcome of it all.

31 December 1993

Another year is drawing to an end. A recent cold snap has made the plight of the homeless more painful. One morning last week, Marc went downstairs for the newspaper and discovered a man sleeping on our porch to get out of the rain. He was wet and wearing only a light jacket. We found one of my no longer used coats to give him as well as some food. Home-lessness grows as public sensitivity to it lessens – except the current bit of hypocritical concern during the Christmas season.

1 January 1994
Complaining foghorns grudgingly usher in another year.

16 March 1994
Several days ago, a body was found tied and stuffed into a shopping cart at Waller and Potomac. Earlier in the month, a body was dumped from a car at Pierce and Waller. After a respite from violent crime in the neighborhood, we now seem deluged by it.

19 March 1994
A beautiful spring day in the park. A bright blue, sunny sky puffed with cotton clouds. The grass is green; the ornamental fruit trees are in bloom, and the sycamores are sending out tentative feelers of green. And people are out to enjoy the sunshine. On the corner of Duboce and Steiner, a sidewalk sale is in progress. The sun worshippers have arrived in the lower end of the park to work on their tans. A group is playing croquet in the central area while dog-owners wander here and there with their pets. Cars hurry to and fro on the streets and the occasional streetcar lumbers in and out of the tunnel. A young man reads a newspaper with its pages spread about him in the grass like large scattered petals. A woman sits on the bench beneath my window looking dejected. Even the beautiful day cannot pull her out of her sadness. But it has worked its magic on the rest of the park.

11 April 1994
Each evening at about five o'clock they begin arriving in the park. It is the gathering of the dog-people. For about two hours they come and go. Some arrive in cars but most walk from their homes. Many have just returned from work and their dogs are bursting with energy after being cooped up all day. It's a varied lot. Most are young and White, middle class suburban youth having their rebellious fling in the city at various edges of the counterculture. Others are older and have lived in the neighborhood for years. The dogs range from prissy poodles to pit bulls and Heinz-variety mutts. They romp and run and wrestle, chase one another and roll in the grass. Their owners are more subdued, some talk to one another, but most do not until their dogs provide vehicles for interaction. I sense that the dogs are the only companions for some of these people, their most intimate

friends and their reasons for living. As dusk settles, they return to apartments that would be painfully empty without their dogs.

2 May 1994

An ongoing legend of the neighborhood claims that a wealthy woman who loved dogs gave Duboce Park to the city as a dog-run. Wishful thinking on the part of the dog-people. History tells us otherwise.

15 May 1994

A nest of blackbirds outside my window.
Greedy babies compete for worms
delivered by their mother.

21 May 1994

Change continues in the neighborhood, a continuation of the pattern I have already noted. I see more young, White professional types, mostly straight – or undecided. Haight Street from the 500 block westward is almost all White now – it was once all Black. The newcomers are mostly young counterculture types paving the way for middle class White professionals. When the projects go, it will probably be the death knell for that element of the Black community. It is still a mixed neighborhood, but it will become increasingly White and probably eventually more Asian. People are discovering that it is one of the more livable neighborhoods of the city – close to downtown, good neighborhood shopping, good weather, and one of the most intact concentrations of Victorian architecture in the city.

I now take the street trees in the neighborhood for granted and must remind myself that when we moved here there were hardly any trees. Even the Duboce Triangle was devoid of trees back then.

23 May 1994

A full moon tonight. We have a beautiful view of the moon from our flat. It rises above Potrero Hill and sails over the park. Sometimes its startling orange surprises the sky and at other times, its chilly whiteness transforms the night into a ghost of the day. Sometimes its delicate sliver of silver hangs in an inky sky. Or its perfectly halved orb is surrounded by envious stars. Duboce Park. A good place for moon-watching.

7 June 1994

During our early years here, the park was filled with Black children of all ages during the late afternoon and evening hours. Almost always a football game was in progress in front of our house. The basketball court was active throughout the evening and into the night. Now hardly any children of any color visit the park. Dogs have replaced them.

13 June 1994

> *A hummingbird sips nectar from diminutive pink blossoms.*
> *A young woman teaches her dingo-like dog acrobatics.*
> *A drummer beats out his madness on a park bench.*
> *A tall thin man dances through the park on stilts.*
> *A gentle wind tosses a rainbow-colored kite.*
> *A flock of blackbirds grazes in the grass.*
> *A streetcar rattles up Duboce Avenue.*
> *A clarinetist wails his sad serenade.*
> *A juggler masters an illusive art.*
> *A June afternoon in the park.*

14 June 1994

A beautiful visitor arrived in the park this morning. A brilliant yellow bird with black wings – perhaps an oriole – rested in the tree outside my window and then flew on to delight other eyes.

24 August 1994

A shirtless young man with long blond hair paces up and down the sidewalk of Duboce Avenue. For over an hour he has paced, obviously waiting for someone. His loneliness and desperation are palpable. Perhaps someone touched him and he is desperately seeking more of that touch. But perhaps the one who touched him is satiated and will not return for more.

30 August 1994

> *A man in the park, wasted by AIDS,*
> *lovingly led by his partner.*
> *If only everyone could be led*
> *to death with such love.*

31 December 1994

A flock of robins arrived in the park this morning. Judging by their plumpness, they fared well at their last stop. Their bright orange breasts add colorful splashes to the bare sycamore branches outside my window.

7 January 1995

Cold, wet, windy storms have blasted the city the past week. I'd forgotten how persistent these storms are, how quickly they follow one another. Wet birds wander the soggy park in search of sustenance. A dozen sea gulls escaped the beaches for our less turbulent park. Dog-owners brave the elements wondering why they didn't settle for goldfish. Howling winds rattle the old house. Streets are flooded. And still another storm lurks offshore. No drought this year.

3 March 1995

Another first for the park – a pet pig! As I walked through the park from Steiner Street this morning, a man carried his pig across the grass. He lovingly set it down, leashed it, and they strolled through the park. After exercising a half-hour, they went home. I've seen pet snakes, rabbits, lizards, parrots, dogs, and cats. And now pigs. What next?

20 March 1995

Such a winter. The rains and winds are relentless and still they come. The park is a quagmire and several park trees have fallen. I was saddened to see an olive tree across the park go down. When we moved here some twenty-three years ago, it was a tall, crooked stick topped with a few leaves struggling to survive. Children tried to climb it, dogs did their thing on it, and an occasional crazy attacked it. But somehow it survived to become a healthy tree, although still an adolescent by slow-growing olive standards. But the recent winds and rains uprooted it and now it is gone. I miss my green friend on the other side of the park.

7 April 1995

A young woman strolls through the park with a pet rat on her shoulder. Having seen the unexpected in the park for so many years, somehow it is expected.

Last weekend a fundraiser for Native Americans with AIDS was held in the park. Many drums accompanied the event. A few drums go a long way when you reside within feet of them.

3 June 1995

During the past few weeks, two large ravens have visited the neighborhood much to the consternation of the feisty little blackbirds that live in the park. Today a group of blackbirds chased the ravens into the air, bombarding them as they flew toward Buena Vista Park. I suspect they were threatening their nests. I have seen the little blackbirds divebomb dogs and people who intrude their domain. Brazen little devils.

24 June 1995

Another evening with Ray at Davies Hospital. Why don't they let him die? No one should suffer such pain and indignity. Death is sometimes a gift. May Ray soon receive his.

28 June 1995

Ray died early this morning. He is free and beyond pain now.

I wonder how many spirits have been released from the burden of life over our little park throughout the years of the hospital? And how many mourners have sought solace in this little green space? Today a few more were added to the list.

1 July 1995

A dog deprived of front legs
kangaroos through the park.

8 July 1995

Today a small herd of stroller-pushing mothers descended on the park. They grazed on packaged food beneath our windows and then moved on.

1 June 1996

Doug Bond, the tenant in our middle flat, is weakening. He has been ill with AIDS for several years now. He is so devoted to the neighborhood. Each Friday before the street sweeper comes, he sweeps all the Potomac sidewalks. He regularly picks up dog-droppings in the park and paints out graffiti on the park restroom and Muni stop. He has filled our garden and sidewalk with pots of bright flowers. On his birthday, a few weeks ago, Marc organized a surprise party and neighbors gathered to let him know how much we appreciate him. He is weakening now and his activities are curtailed. He is a fine man. If he is not memorialized elsewhere, may this serve as his memorial.

10 June 1996

The public housing projects on Haight Street are empty and awaiting demolition. They were breeding grounds for crime and violence, and everyone is hoping for great changes now that they are gone.

92

Periodically boys climb onto the roof of the park restroom and strut their stuff. After realizing it's no great conquest, they soon descend and resume their play. Occasionally, they cling to the rear attachment of the streetcars and ride through the tunnel. I suspect boys have done that since the first streetcars entered the tunnel.

22 June 1996

The late, lingering evening of summer solstice.
A mellow time to watch unremarkable happenings in the park.

28 June 1996

The remodeling of the little store at Potomac and Waller is almost completed. Someone has put big bucks into it. It will be a mortgage brokerage office. Throughout the history of Potomac Street it has been a Mom and Pop store: that says something about the changing character of the neighborhood.

1 July 1996

Unusually hot weather for San Francisco. Some call it earthquake weather. In fact, we had a small quake last night.

A young girl is capitalizing on the heat wave by selling lemonade in the park under the shade of a tree. Dog biscuits are also included in her menu. A future CEO.

7 December 1996

The projects on Haight Street are gone. All that remains is an empty, muddy scar surrounded by derelict Victorian buildings.

17 December 1996

A gothic day complete with howling winds
and somber gray skies.
Melancholy weather
with a touch of morbidity.

13 May 1997

Sea gulls no longer come to the park in stormy weather. Too many dogs.

6 June 1997

A small group of Potomac Street residents are currently collecting signatures from property owners requesting PG&E to underground the overhead wires. We need fifty percent of the property owners on Potomac, the first block of Pierce and the two blocks of Waller between Steiner and Scott. We have the signatures for Potomac and Pierce, and are working on Waller Street. Absentee property-owners, of course, are the ones refusing to sign.

New streetcars are test-running on the tracks, the third set I have watched from my windows. When we moved here, the old green cars wiggled up and down Duboce Avenue. They were replaced by sleek, orange and white cars. And now, twenty years later, they are giving way to new red and gray state-of-the-art cars. Will I live to see another fleet of streetcars?

9 June 1997

If one feels lonely, the front steps are a good place to go. Before long, someone says "hello" or a neighbor stops to chat. The park offers entertaining diversions too – perhaps a dog-fight, a juggler practicing his art, or someone feeding a rat to his pet snake. Cars come and go and before you know it, an hour has passed and the loneliness is gone.

18 January 1998

Some sad news. Christina Jobst, our neighbor across the park at 69 Duboce Avenue is selling her home and moving into more manageable quarters. She is in her early 80s and has lived in her house and slept in the same bedroom since she was four years old. Until recently, she still drove the 1947 Plymouth which she bought new. The house is in mint condition and will make someone a lovely home.

The store front at the end of Potomac Street is currently occupied by a lesbian press called Cleis, a highly regarded small press. It is a good addition to the street, quiet and operated by pleasant people.

18 February 1998

> *Cruel, cold rains*
> *for those who live on the streets.*

9 May 1998

I increasingly feel like a stranger in this neighborhood. It has become so youthful. I now understand claims I once heard from old people who told me that young people look through them as if they do not exist. Youth –

a mere blink in the journey through life. Yet we have elevated it as the model for all things, a model often unattainable for even the young.

24 May 1998

Another Potomac Street neighbor will soon be moving. Mrs. Douglas who has lived at 70 Potomac since the early 1950s is selling her house and moving into a retirement home. She is 84 and her family was one of the first Black families to move to the street. Her husband died in the house where most of her ten children were raised. Only four children are now living, three having died in the last two years. Despite the many tragedies of her life, she maintains a happy front to the world with a warm smile and a friendly hello. She was once a large, robust woman, but now she is thin and needs a cane to get about. Real estate vultures and others are hovering about her house hoping to steal it away. Another Black family gone from the street. When we moved here almost the entire street was Black. Now only one family remains – plus Marc and a widow who lives next door.

"Friends of Duboce Park" has regrouped and this time it appears something might happen since the group has the backing of the new assistant park director and the Duboce Triangle Neighborhood Association. Concerns are the usual ones – maintenance of trees, sprinkler problems, dog-droppings, off-leashes, and barking. I've seen so many of these groups come and go. I'm afraid I'm a bit burnt-out on park matters.

5 July 1998

Dog people are weird.

I heard a woman sitting on a park bench say: "Bad doggy. You jumped up and got Mama's booby all dirty."

Another hosted a birthday party in the park for her dog, complete with balloons, games, and treats for all dogs in attendance.

Then there was the woman who routinely masturbated her dog on the park bench because it gave him "pleasure."

And the man who dressed his two dogs in blue jeans and plaid shirts.

And the one who dyed his dog's tail the same purple as his own pony tail.

And the one who rigged an umbrella on his dog on rainy days.

And the one whose yellow raincoat matched the raincoat of his dog.

And the one who hired jazz musicians to play at her dog's birthday pool-party.

I rest my case.

Dog people are weird.

21 September 1998

A tiny hummingbird pauses in midair outside my window.
How does such fragile delicacy survive in such a harsh world?
Perhaps the delicacy is tougher than I realize
or
perhaps the world is not as harsh as I think.

1 October 1998

A few years ago, a coffeehouse called "Bean There" opened at the corner of Waller and Steiner. Owned and operated by two brothers, it is a wonderful addition to the neighborhood and certainly convenient for satiating my caffeine needs. With indoor and outdoor seating, it accommodates a lively neighborhood crowd. An always-changing corps of youthful workers behind the counter serves the diverse collection of hipsters, firemen, seniors, students, young parents with babies, and other neighborhood regulars who patronize the place. I prefer sitting outdoors where I can watch the parade of pedestrians, dogs, and vehicular traffic. It has become somewhat of a neighborhood gathering place and invariably one runs into a friend, an acquaintance, a familiar face, or a warm smile. And the occasional weirdo.

12 October 1998

Doug is in the hospital. The HIV virus has taken his left eye. His doctor is pumping yet another drug into him. He has become withdrawn, angry and bitter. Not the Doug of better days we all knew and loved. How many more friends will this horrible disease claim? With each friend who survives the disease a long time, I think maybe he will be the one who beats it. But none do.

31 December 1998

A tragedy on our little street. Two days before Christmas, the son of Mrs. Genette Trammell was murdered in his home on Third Street. Not a happy Christmas for that family. The son suffered a difficult life – prison, drugs, and the sad litany of so many inner-city young Black men. This is Mrs. Trammell's third child who has been murdered. After being beaten by life so brutally so many times, one wonders how she can face each new day. A tremendously strong woman.

Beneath the tough exterior she has needed to survive is a kind, sensitive woman who has raised countless numbers of grandchildren, great-grandchildren, and great-great-grandchildren. A few years ago, a homeless White woman lived in the park and occasionally slept on the Potomac

Street sidewalks. While others called the police to get rid of her, Mrs. Trammell offered her food, use of her bathroom, and storage on her porch. A kind heart beats beneath that tough exterior.

1 January 1999

A sunny morning and a park full of robins.
A promising beginning
for a new year.

15 April 1999

"Brownie Mary" died recently. She earned her name from the marijuana-laced brownies she baked and sold from her flat on Walter Street. I first heard of her when she was arrested in 1981 for the illegal sale of marijuana. She was placed on probation and eventually became an activist for the legalization of medical marijuana, especially after it proved effective in alleviating the suffering of AIDS patients. She continued baking pot-laced brownies and made the headlines each time she was arrested. She eventually became a poster-child for the legalization of medical marijuana as well as a beloved icon in the gay community. Another colorful neighborhood character is gone.

8 August 1999

So long since I have written in this journal. I've been busy with other writing projects and obviously not sufficiently inspired to share my thoughts with the journal. Three weeks ago a streetcar struck me as I was crossing Duboce Avenue at Steiner. I escaped with a badly broken leg and lots of time to stare at the walls of this flat – and to count the steps as I maneuver them on crutches from the sidewalk to the top floor.

Yesterday sidewalk trees were planted along the park at Steiner and Scott. More green is always welcomed.

Haight Street continues to turn around. The new public housing in the 300 block is finished and neighboring houses are being renovated. The old Haight Street theater will become condominiums. Restaurants and other businesses come and go, some remain. The neighborhood is increasingly mainstream and new property owners are increasingly straight White couples who plan to stay around with their children. We'll see.

13 August 1999

Two houses on the street were recently purchased by young African Americans. The Douglas house was bought by a man who is slowly restoring it and the Dilly house was bought by a young couple who had their first child shortly after moving in. They are middle class professionals and quite different from the Black population that lived here when we arrived. It's good to see African Americans returning to the neighborhood.

15 August 1999

Yesterday the park hosted a gathering supporting the medical use of marijuana. I certainly support the medical use of marijuana, but I'm afraid much of the crowd used the event to get high – marijuana was only one of the many ways. Stands pushing various political agendas populated the lower park where loudspeakers blasted music of dubious merit. Several hundred people were gathered. It was a good day to vacate the house – and we did.

17 August 1999

Two young medical research physicists live in the bottom flat. They rescue white rats from their labs and provide them homes until they pass on to the rat-hereafter. Their little corpses are then buried in the park beside the house by their mourning benefactors. In the event some future archaeologists discover an inexplicably large number of rat bones in the park beside the house, they now know their origin.

9 September 1999

Lightning struck the Johnck house across the street from us. It knocked bricks from the chimney, blew out computers, televisions, and telephones. Two computers were damaged in our building. A freak storm.

6 October 1999

We lost a tree on Potomac Street. New tenants were moving into the building next door and as they entered Potomac with their rental truck, they hit and toppled an acacia tree at the entrance. Not a good way to impress new neighbors.

5 March 2000

Potomac Street is currently under excavation for a new sewer line. The street looks like a war zone and residents are none too happy that it is off-limits to their cars.

20 December 2000

The neighborhood continues to change. A house on Potomac Street sold for over a million dollars! Who would have guessed that our tough little street would become one of the desirable neighborhoods of the city? We attended a neighborhood gathering last week where the majority of the men wore tuxedoes. There was a time not long ago when I felt overdressed in blue jeans at neighborhood affairs. The neighborhood and the city have changed so much. At times I feel like a stranger in both.

31 January 2001

Morning fog against the windows.
A soft, fuzzy world punctuated by moaning foghorns.

21 April 2001

Today is the centennial celebration of the founding of Duboce Park. The centennial date was actually last September, but the committee in charge wanted to wait for the completion of the new playground before celebrating. Such is completed and after days of rain, sunshine greets the several hundred celebrants in the park.

Events include a display of historic photos, balloon sculptures, antique cars, a fire truck, a police car, a stilt walker, and various play activities for children. A stand announcing "Free Doggy Chiropractic" takes care of certain canine needs. Mayor Willie Brown is scheduled to appear later in the day.

24 April 2001

Doug is very ill. He has fought AIDS for a long time and now the end is drawing near. He was recently diagnosed with lymphoma cancer and began chemotherapy, but after two chemo infusions, he worsened so badly the treatment was discontinued. Chemo is a terrible treatment. Future generations will be horrified that we once did that to ones we love.

6 October 2001

The sad events of September 11 continue to disturb the nation and a good part of the world. I was in Washington, D.C. when the Pentagon was attacked a few blocks from where I was staying. What a species we are. We have created a technology that increasingly understands the animating forces of the universe, but yet we have this primitive need to kill and destroy one another. And now we are bombing Afghanistan.

14 October 2001

Children have returned to the neighborhood with a vengeance. Where did they come from so quickly? I think the new playground has attracted some from outside the neighborhood. I have a feeling they are here to stay. These parents will not flee to the suburbs when their children reach school age. But probably their kids will flee the city when they reach adulthood to escape their demanding, helicopter parents. The beat goes on.

25 December 2001

A bird in a barren tree outside my window
silhouetted against a gray sky.
Merry Christmas.

3 June 2002

I don't hear the foghorns anymore. I was told they have been replaced by computers that now guide ships into the bay. I miss their mournful, distant wails, a comforting assurance that someone was watching over the foggy bay.

12 July 2002

PG&E is finally undergrounding the overhead wires on Potomac Street. What a mess. Dust and dirt everywhere.

11 August 2002

A death on the street. Zoya Sheedy, who lived twenty-five years at 74 Potomac Street, died following surgery at UCSF hospital. Zoya was a beloved member of the neighborhood and will be missed by many. A New Yorker of Russian immigrant parents, she never lost her New York speech and projected a tough New York exterior that protected a sensitive, vulnerable interior. She loved dogs and people and over the years she had a big collection of both. Several times a day she visited the park with her dogs and was one of the most familiar figures in the neighborhood. Shortly before she moved to Potomac Street, an accident resulted in the amputation of her left leg. However, it never slowed her down and only occasionally dampened her spirits. She traveled the world, attended theater, symphony, opera, and the ballet. She was always ready to try something new and celebrated her 80th birthday with a hot-air balloon ride.

At her request, she was cremated. A memorial service was held for her in the park followed by a gathering of about seventy-five people in our flat. A memorial plaque will be placed on a park bench in her name and a tree planted in the playground in her memory. Many will miss Zoya Sheedy. She was a rare edition. They don't make them like her anymore.

Another death on the street: Mr. Fred Ubungen, a 92-year-old Filipino neighbor, died of a stroke a few days after Zoya's death. He had lived on the street since the late 1940s, probably the first non-White property owner on Potomac Street. He was a quiet, kindly man of few words. His gentle presence will be missed.

14 August 2004

Doug died today.

17 October 2004

Last night I was returning home from the opera at midnight when I encountered two raccoons leisurely strolling down Potomac Street. They paused at the park entrance and then wandered uphill. They were a refreshing reminder that some animals have survived the human incursion into their space.

9 January 2005

Finally the undergrounding of wires on Potomac Street is completed. Eight years ago, we began circulating neighborhood petitions for the event. The ugly cluttered masses of wires are gone and only the poles remain. What a difference!

The neighborhood continues in the direction it has moved for some years. Increasingly, only the well-heeled can afford to live here. After purchase, properties are frequently renovated into even more expensive dwellings. Single family homes sell for a million dollars or more. Will that seem like a bargain someday? Probably.

23 February 2005

Today the last utility pole was removed from Potomac Street! Finally! No more ugly wires and poles. The street looks cleaner and more expansive.

5 July 2005

More Asians are moving into the neighborhood. Filipinos have lived on the street for many years, but now Chinese young people are beginning to move in. I suspect that someday this neighborhood will be predominantly Chinese as has happened elsewhere in the city. I welcome the Chinese neighbors, but I like my neighborhoods ethnically mixed – hopefully, that mix will continue in this one.

17 October 2005

Seagulls, children, and sunbathers are gone from the park. Only dogs now.

4 February 2006

Finally, the Potomac Street project is concluded. Today, the old patched surface of the street was removed and replaced with a new one. During the past ten years, a new sewer line was installed, water lines were replaced, and the overhead wires were undergrounded. Each, of course, was a separate operation which tore up the street and disrupted traffic and covered everything with fine dust. Now the project is finished. A few years late, but a promising new face for Potomac Street's entry into the 21st Century.

Dennis Tomason who lived at 73 Potomac Street died last week. He called me the day before Christmas and said he was ill and asked if I would take him to the emergency room at California Pacific Medical Center across the park. I did so, and his condition deteriorated rapidly. He was soon in a coma and for a month survived on life-support equipment. Another AIDS death. It is not over yet.

30 November 2006

> *Two saucy, sassy ravens strutting down Potomac Street*
> *cawing raucously: "Get out of our way!"*

15 January 2007

Construction will soon begin for yet another hospital reincarnation across the park. First, German Hospital, then Franklin Hospital, then Ralph K. Davies Medical Center, and then California Pacific Medical Center. What next?

26 March 2007

> *Bursting in white, the Potomac plum tree*
> *blizzards its blossoms down the street*
> *on gusty March winds.*
> *Passers-by stop and marvel.*

22 May 2007

An old friend died today. The park department cut down the tree outside my window. It was a shrub when we moved here, but over the years it grew almost as tall as our house. Each year, it shared small white flowers with bees and hosted birds' nests in its limbs. In recent years it began slowly

102

dying, a limb at a time. And now it is gone. I grew old with my green friend. I miss its leafy companionship.

1 June 2007

Today I glanced out my window and was greeted by a green and red parrot perched on a tree branch, the only parrot I've ever seen in Duboce Park. Maybe it escaped its cage, or perhaps it is a renegade from the Telegraph Hill flock.

20 June 2007

> *Outside my window,*
> *a young man on stilts*
> *dances to a drummer*
> *different from mine.*

3 July 2007

An explosion of babies in the neighborhood! Balloon-bellied women navigating the sidewalks, toddlers in the park, strollers everywhere, and nursing mothers in the coffeehouses. The latest invasion. Will they replace the dogs? I doubt it.

10 September 2007

Rarely do I look into the park and find no one there. No matter the time of day or night, someone is walking a dog, sitting in the grass, waiting for a streetcar, hurrying to some destination, playing a musical instrument, reading a book, flying a kite, prancing on stilts, exercising a snake, or simply sitting on a bench and watching the world go by.

17 October 2007

The neighborhood has so many more vehicles than in the years when we first moved here. Streets were quiet and relatively empty then; now they are rarely empty and finding street-parking at night is often an exercise in futility.

6 November 2007

Yet again the park is undergoing renovation. And yet again, more green space is eaten away by intrusions into the grass. Over the years, the Sunset Tunnel, the Harvey Milk Recreation Center, the basketball court, the playground, and the labyrinth have taken their toll on the green space of the park – and now additional sidewalks and recreation space for the dog-people. The current project will include a swag-chain enclosed space at the lower end of the park for dogs while the upper park will be reserved for humans and their offspring. It all seems an exercise in futility, not to mention a waste of money. If they believe the dog-crowd will confine their canines to the enclosed area, I have a bridge I'll sell them.

Will the park one day be a concrete slab? At this rate, perhaps so.

20 November 2007

During the current construction in the park, the entrance to Potomac Street is blocked by a metal fence covered with a screen. An inconvenience for those of us who live at this end of the street, but an unexpected plus because it has altered the wind patterns that normally blow all papers and leaves from the street to the front of our house. I am enjoying the respite from sweeping the sidewalk.

7 December 2007

Pearl Harbor Day. Each year it means less to more people.

10 December 2007

I wonder how many different species of birds visit Duboce Park. Throughout the years I have regularly seen hummingbirds, robins, blackbirds, ravens, finches, sparrows, pigeons, and blue jays. Rare visitors include an oriole and a parrot. Before the invasion of dogs, many sea gulls visited the park during stormy weather at the beaches. I have seen a few other birds I could not identify.

15 December 2007

Sometimes when I walk through the neighborhood, I encounter ghosts from the past: Sylvia's wonderful laugh, Black kids playing football in the park, the empty lots where houses now stand, the Red Sisters depositing their garbage in a park trash can, the old green streetcars swaying and clattering up Duboce Avenue, hundreds of Blacks gathered on Haight Street in the late afternoon, Zoya and her dogs holding court on a park bench, frightened neighbors clustered in the park after the '89 earthquake, the bells that pealed three times a day in the church across the park, Doug and his little dog Billy-Bob sweeping the sidewalks, the grungy pool hall where a Thai restaurant now serves the in-people, the Black store-front churches at the intersection of Waller and Steiner rocking the neighborhood with their Sunday morning services, a cold February morning when the park was white with snow, hookers from Haight Street yelling for Stella to throw down the key, Albert playing his saxophone in the park, and the smell of barbecued chicken from the Two Sisters store at the end of Potomac Street.

All are ghosts now, ushering me from the past into an uncertain future where I shall someday join them.

31 December 2007

I await the next chapter.

2016 Afterword

SINCE I COMPLETED this book in 2007, many of the trends I noted at that time for Potomac Street and the Lower Haight have continued.

Visually, the neighborhood continues to improve although a long-time neighbor bemoaned that the Victorian houses are increasingly painted in conservative tones compared to the brilliant colors that once brightened the streets. Scaffolding is scattered throughout the neighborhood as fresh paint jobs and renovations prepare the houses for another hundred years. Many residents have created attractive potted gardens on their sidewalks and planted drought-tolerant plants in the small spaces fronting their homes. More street trees shade the sidewalks and it is sometimes difficult for me to remember that hardly any street trees were found when I moved here in 1972. The Lower Haight has become a very "in" neighborhood with its excellent public transportation, convenience to downtown, intact Victorian architecture, good restaurants, sunny weather, and proximity to the Castro, Upper Haight, Mission, and Upper Market.

The city recently designated the Duboce Park neighborhood (including Potomac Street) a historic district bordered by Steiner Street, Waller Street, Scott Street, and Duboce Avenue. This designation dictates that the exteriors of the buildings cannot be altered (except to restore them to their original designs) but few restrictions apply to the interiors so long as they conform to city codes. The late Victorian interiors are currently out of fashion and consequently buildings that sold for one or two million dollars are then gutted of their Victorian décor, sometimes costing an additional million to become part of the current fashion. The so-called "great room" which combines several traditional room spaces into a single large unified space seems the design choice for many renovators. Probably the next generation will spend small fortunes to restore the Victorian interiors, but such is the nature of fashion.

I no longer claim that rents and real estate prices cannot possibly go higher in the neighborhood (and the city) but they have and probably will continue to do so, driven upward by the critical housing shortage in this expanding city as well as the well-heeled youth – many from Silicon Valley and mostly White – who can afford them. Eager to be part of the San Francisco legend, they seek an excitement they find lacking in the Valley where they work and the suburbs where many of them grew up. Young Asians, probably mostly Chinese, are a growing presence among this crowd. Prices at local restaurants and Mom and Pop stores are climbing to match the high salaries of some of the newcomers. But many of these little stores have disappeared, unable to afford the new rents. San Francisco was recently declared the most expensive city in the United States, hardly something warranting pride. The neighborhood is becoming increasingly affluent, White and Asian. Rents have skyrocketed and sale prices are even more astronomical. A six-room flat on nearby Waller Street in a newly renovated building is currently on the rental market for $8,600 monthly. Some buildings that sold well below $50,000 when I moved to the neighborhood now sell for one to three million dollars. Can this insanity continue? Surely not, but I've said that before.

Many of the newcomers seek the neighborhood for its edge and vitality that ironically their very presence is slowly dulling. Many old timers blame the so-called "Techies," youthful Millennials who dominate the Silicon Valley booming tech industry, for the many changes they perceive as undesirable. But the Techies are simply doing what youth has always done, flocking to places where their own kind gathers. I behaved similarly when I was young, albeit in a considerably different socio-economic milieu. They tread the sidewalks zombie-like, addicted to their smartphones while pushing baby strollers or walking dogs. Sleek, phantom-like busses slip through the early morning streets quietly gathering them, delivering them to jobs in Silicon Valley and returning them home in the early evening hours. High boots and tight pants are the current regimental wear for the young women while their male counterparts favor low-slung trousers (but not low enough to be saggers) and beards of various persuasions. Tattoos and piercings seem optional.

The growing population of babies and children in the neighborhood is a refreshing presence that brings smiles to people who otherwise rarely smile. Local news stories occasionally claim that families with children are leaving San Francisco and that the city has the lowest child-per-capita of any major city in the United States. Such is certainly not evident in this neighborhood. Young White people who moved to the city for jobs in the expanding economy are staying to raise their families, rejecting the suburbs of their childhood. Potomac Street has sixteen children at last count, the highest in recent history. Two children, one dog and a Latina nanny seem prerequisites for living in the neighborhood these days. Ideally the children are enrolled in a private school and an immersion language program – French for the status-conscious parents, Chinese and Spanish for the pragmatic ones. Molding their offspring into the images they have chosen, these parents keep a hopeful eye toward the Ivy League schools back East.

For many years, Lower Haight Street has been popular among the counterculture youth. It is still a hangout for youth, but a very different kind of youth who can afford the prices and rents. The number of Blacks in the city continues to decline and that trend is reflected in the Lower Haight. Only two Black businesses of the old days remain on Haight Street: Two Jacks, a seafood restaurant, and Café International, a coffeehouse that sponsors poetry readings, live music and shows by local artists. Among the colorful names of other current Haight Street shops and restaurants are Love N Haight, Silky Touch, Haight to Wash, Mythic Pizza, Blown Away, Mad Dog in the Fog, Idle Hands, Molotov's, and Noc Noc. The street's restaurants reflect the ethnic diversity of the city and include Syrian, Japanese, Chinese, Vietnamese, Indian, Korean, Thai, Mexican, Ethiopian, and Salvadorian cuisine as well as such American staples as soul food, southern barbecue, pizza, and sandwiches. I recently counted thirty restaurants within three blocks of my Duboce Park home, the majority of them on Haight Street. In addition, numerous small shops offer manicures, haircuts, music, flowers, clothing, and gift items. Various murals brighten formerly blank walls, a trend found throughout the city.

Certain San Francisco neighborhoods, such as North Beach, have always hosted coffeehouses but in recent years they have become ubiquitous throughout the city, providing local gathering places for neighbors. Several are scattered throughout the Lower Haight and many residents have their favorite haunt. They are populated mostly by young people seemingly seeking the company of one another but rarely interacting beyond their laptops.

The city bemoans the departure of its artists, many of whom have left for more affordable spaces in the East Bay. Potomac Street is no exception. During my early years in the neighborhood, dancers, painters, musicians, writers, actors, singers and other artists populated Potomac Street; today I know only four artists on the street.

Crime is down considerably from the early days, but we are far from crime-free; household burglaries, muggings, car break-ins and even the occasional murder are not uncommon in the neighborhood. A few months ago there was a rash of thefts by young men brazenly stealing smartphones from the hands of people walking the streets engrossed in their devices.

Most of the gas stations and empty lots on nearby upper Market Street are gone, replaced by large residential complexes of dubious aesthetics, adding hundreds more to the increasingly dense population of the neighborhood. So far we have been spared the highrise buildings that congest the old downtown.

The stretch of Duboce Avenue from the Sunset Tunnel to the downtown tunnel at Church Street has been renovated with new Muni rails, new streetlights, new waiting platforms and new planters. A current project is replacing the rails in the tunnel, much to the chagrin of local drivers denied parking along the park-side of the street because of the construction equipment.

Duboce Park has never looked better during the time I have lived here. Apparently White voices are better heard at City Hall. An additional playground and a labyrinth have been added to the upper park. Scores of dogs, the significant others of many people, visit the park daily. They are mostly confined to the lower half of the park and for the most part, dog owners (now called "dog guardians" in politically correct San Francisco) pick up after their animals and the old name "Dog Shit Park" belongs to the past – although the "guardians" still engage in occasional screaming bouts with one another about doggy misdeeds. Small dogs are the current preference, perhaps because they fit more easily into the smaller living spaces of the new construction. But a petite woman I sometimes see in the park defies this trend with her huge Great Dane, seemingly large enough for her to saddle and roundup the other canines in the park.

For nine years, a celebration called Dog Fest has annually feted dogs in Duboce Park. Each year it grows larger. People bring their dogs and children to the park which is filled with booths and activities catering to both. Dogs compete for Best Trick, Best Costume, Best Ears, Best Bark and more. It is packed and needless to say it is noisy, a day I choose to be away from home. The proceeds from the event go to nearby McKinley Elementary School. This year over $100,000 was raised.

The Harvey Milk Center continues to dominate the upper park, but a recent renovation resulted in a much more attractive building. New landscaping is established around the Center and throughout the park resulting in flowering trees and bushes most of the year. Our little green space is greatly used, especially on sunny weekends when people fill the park with their picnics, games, children, dogs and assorted antics.

A new bike lane, called "The Wiggle," snakes up Duboce Avenue from Market Street, turns right onto Steiner, left onto Waller, and then right again at Pierce to destinations beyond. A shop on nearby Waller Street conducts a brisk business selling and repairing bicycles. More bikes seem to appear each week, adding to the growing daytime congestion of the once empty neighborhood streets. Cars and bicycles are grudgingly learning to accommodate one another. Most are responsible and respectful, but the occasional driver or cyclist screams obscenities and curses at some perceived offender.

Homelessness is an ongoing problem in this very affluent city which somehow the city coffers and administrators are unable to solve. Potomac is no exception. One recent morning I walked down the street and saw three people sleeping on sidewalks and in doorways. Some go to the park for respite from the sidewalks until someone calls the police who escort them away from the sensitive eyes of the neighborhood.

San Francisco is growing by leaps and bounds. According to a recent news report, ten thousand people moved to the city last year. I miss that small-town city I first embraced almost fifty years ago, but like it or not that city is gone. A new San Francisco is evolving and hopefully that new city will retain some of the soul and spirit that made the old San Francisco such a very special place.

PART THREE

APPENDICES

Appendix One

An Outline of the Legal History of Duboce Park

From *Real Estate Owned by the City and County of San Francisco and Historical Data Relating to Same, With Citations From Decisions of the Superior, Supreme and Federal Courts in Relation to Land Titles Vested in the Municipality.* Published by Authority Resolution #3593 (New Series) of the Board of Supervisors of the City and County of San Francisco. July 1, 1909. Pp. 91-92.

The following excerpts from the above volume outline the legal history of the land that is now Duboce Park.

1. "The original reserve for Hospital Purposes under the provisions of the Van Ness Ordinance (Order No. 822) and Order No. 845 (See Appendix, Municipal Reports 1867-68, pp. 588, 590, 591), included all the land bounded by Waller street, Duboce Avenue (formerly Ridley st. and later 13th st.), Scott and Steiner streets."

2. "In Fourth District Court, Cause No. 11, 491 and 14,511, May 20, 1869, Mary Polack recovered, and partition was made setting off another portion of the lot to her and the remaining portion described to the city and county.

"Mary Polack vs. City and County of San Francisco, Fourth District, No. 14,511. Suit for Partition.

"On December 7, 1868, the Court appointed George C. Potter, Thomas Young and Joseph S. Paxson referees to divide the property and allot the several portions to the parties hereto according to the respective rights of plaintiff and defendant. On February 12, 1869, the referees made their report and filed the same, accompanied by a map, with the Court. On May 20, 1869, the report was confirmed by the Court and it was ordered, adjudged and decreed that the plaintiff shall be the owner in fee simple of the land bounded and described as follows:

"'Commencing at the southwest corner of Waller and Steiner streets; thence south on the west line of Steiner street 316 feet; thence at right angles west 434 feet to a point in the line described in said Order; thence in a north-westerly direction along said line to a point distant 25 feet east of the east line of Scott street; thence east on the south line of Waller street to the point of beginning.'"

"Recorded June 1, 1869, Book H. page 484. Vide Decision of Supreme Court in City and County of San Francisco vs. Honora Sharp, 125 Cal., page 534."

3. "In 12th District Court, Jan. 17, 1873, title quieted against the city and county in favor of Dan Rogers to a portion of this lot (Cause #9915)."

4. After losing part of the "hospital" land in the above court cases, the city retained the following portion of the land:

"Commencing at a point on the westerly line of Steiner street, distant thereon 316 feet from southerly line of Waller street; running thence westerly and parallel with 13th street (now Duboce avenue) 434 feet; thence in a northerly direction to a point distant 25 feet east of the easterly line of Scott street, 265 feet south of the southerly line of Waller street, running thence northeasterly to a point on said southerly line of Waller street 63 feet easterly from the easterly line of Scott street; thence westerly along said south line of Waller street 63 feet; thence southerly along the easterly line of Scott street 458.01/8 feet to the northerly line of 13th street [now Duboce avenue]; thence easterly along said northerly line of 13th street [now Duboce avenue] 896 feet 10 inches to the westerly line of Steiner street; thence northerly along said westerly line of Steiner street 216 feet to the point of commencement."

5. "Leased to the 'San Francisco Female Hospital' for a term of three years at a nominal rent of $1.00 per year from April, 1880. Vide Resolution No. 14,564 (New Series)."

6. "On May 26, 1896, the City and County brought action against Honora Sharp (No. 55, 323, Superior Court), Eliza M. Sharp, et al. (No 55, 334, Superior Court), and German Savings and Loan Society, et al. (No. 54, 305, Superior Court) to quiet its title to several described parcels of land included within the boundaries of the above described lot. Judgment in the favor of the City and County was rendered in all of these cases. (Municipal Reports 1896-97, pp. 370, 371). In action No. 55, 323, the defendant, Honora Sharp appealed to the Supreme Court, (S.F. No. 1206, Department 8) where the judgment of the lower court was affirmed (185 Cal. 536)."

7. "On April 16, 1897, the City and County brought an action against John H. Dunham et al. (No. 59, 103, Superior Court) to quiet its title to the above described parcel of land. On May 25, 1897, motion for judgment on the pleadings was granted and the judgment was entered for plaintiff as prayed for. (Municipal Reports 1896-97, p. 387). From this judgment the defendants appealed to the Supreme Court, November 18, 1897, (Municipal Reports 1897-98, p. 705). The Supreme Court affirmed the judgment of the lower court on the authority of San Francisco v. Sharp, supra. (125 Cal. XIX)."

8. "Pursuant to Ordinance No. 42, April 13, 1900, the remaining portion of the Hospital Lot was dedicated as a public park, named and designated 'Duboce Park,' and placed under the exclusive control and management of the Board of Park Commissioners to be maintained by said Board."

9. "Pursuant to Ordinance No. 139, September 8, 1900, the above portion of the Hospital Lot (which was by Ordinance No. 42, April 13, 1900, dedicated for public park purposes) was named and designated 'Duboce Park.'

Appendix Two

Duboce Park Dedication

(From the *San Francisco Chronicle*, Monday, September 10, 1900, page 9)

DEDICATION OF DUBOCE PARK

AN UNSIGHTLY TRACT TO BE BEAUTIFIED

FITTING CEREMONIES ARE HELD IN MEMORY OF A GALLANT SOLDIER

MAYOR PHELAN AND RABBI VOORSANGER CONGRATULATE THE
RESIDENTS OF THE DISTRICT IN HAPPY WORDS

Duboce Park was dedicated yesterday morning, and in a short time another unsightly portion of the city will be a thing of the past and be replaced with green sward and flowering shrubs to delight the eye and add to the healthfulness and beauty of the city.

Duboce Park is situated on the northern and western slope of the hill surmounted by what is known as Buena Vista park. It lies two blocks long on Thirteenth street and is a block wide. It is bounded on one end by Scott and on the other by Steiner. The tract of land has long been a bone of contention, and, cut down one-half of its original size through litigation, it goes to a purpose akin to what was originally intended.

Forty years ago the land was set apart as a site for a public hospital. Taxes became due on the property, which was finally involved in litigation with the German Savings Bank and the Sharp estate as claimants against the city for the property. One-half of it was finally captured by the bank and the city retained a half. The land has been used as an Italian vegetable garden and later by A. E. Buckman, the contractor, as a dumping ground for rock and for stables.

Through the efforts of the New Park Improvement Club the ramshackle buildings were condemned as a nuisance and the site was cleared of everything but the large quantities of rock that litter the surface of the ground. For the purpose of improvement $1500 was raised by the club and $5000 has been appropriated by the Board of Supervisors.

The exercises yesterday were in keeping with the purpose for which they were intended, partly as a rejoicing by the residents of the district for a victory for which they had long striven, and partly to give popular sanction to the commemoration of a gallant California soldier in naming the park in honor of the late Colonel Duboce.

114

National airs were played by the First Regiment Band, while on a gaily decorated stand erected in the center of the plot of ground and near a newly erected flagpole were President E. C. Prieber of the New Park Improvement Club, Mayor James D. Phelan, Rabbi Voorsanger, Chief of Police Sullivan, Captain Seymour and the officers of the First California regiment. Nearly 1500 people had gathered about the stand when President Prieber introduced Mayor Phelan to the gathering.

The Mayor, in a short address, congratulated the people of the district on converting the barren piece of land into a park. He said: "For some reason the city has lost one-half the piece of land that it originally had, but is fortunate in getting the other half. It is better as a park than as a hospital, for which it was originally intended, for the one conduces to health of the community, while the most the other can do is to restore it. The people have been wise enough at this time to set apart for a park this piece of land, which at the present time looks as if it had been the scene of a battle among the gods in which they threw huge rocks at one another."

He then paid a glowing tribute to the gallant Colonel for whom the park was named, in which he voiced the sentiment that he could not think of a more appropriate way in which to commemorate the memory of a patriot who died for his country.

After the playing of "Columbia," Rabbi Voorsanger was introduced, and directed the attention of the people to the ethical side of such a movement as that which prompted the residents to wish for a park in their midst. "Home," he said, "is an old Anglo-Saxon word that means more than a mere lodging place where one eats and sleeps. It means a place where all that tends to the culture of the mind, as well as the body, is situated. Parks, clubs, churches and all public places go to make up home and tend to the higher culture, which, as it develops, will require more of them." He told the people not to forget the old Roman precept, that it was good to die for one's country, and he likened Duboce to the soldier in the old Saxon fable, who "turned his face toward the skies and climbed the ladder of the immortals."

Upon the closing of the speech the band played the "Star-Spangled Banner," and a new flag was unfurled from the peak of the flagpole. The buglers from Army and Navy Parlor, No. 207, of the Native Sons of the Golden West, sounded the calls, while members of Olympus Parlor, No. 189, attended to the raising of the flag.

Appendix Three
Potomac Street Residents in 1900, 1910, 1920, 1930, and 1940

The United States Censuses of 1900, 1910, 1920, 1930, and 1940 report the following names as residents of Potomac Street (called Portola Street until 1927). The street addresses are followed by the names of occupants. A household head is indicated in the third column and the relationship of others in the household to him or her is also indicated in that column. Note that some multiple family households have more than one head. The ages of household members are in the last column. The careful reader will notice inconsistencies in some of the households; the data are, however, as they appear in the census reports. A question mark in parentheses (?) following a name indicates an uncertain spelling due to the poor penmanship of the census-taker. Because of the seventy-two year seal on certain census data, names are unavailable for the 1950 and subsequent censuses.

1900 Potomac Street Residents

Address	Name	Relation	Age
56	Moore, George	Head	45
	Moore, Charlotte	Wife	43
	Moore, Kenneth	Son	1
	Fulton, Morton	Boarder	20
	Cuthburt, Rose	Servant	53
57	MacKenzie, Mansfield	Head	23
	MacKenzie, Blanche	Wife	20
	Hamilton, Forrest	Boarder	14
60	Bepler, Frederick	Head	38
	Bepler, Charlotte	Wife	32
	Bepler, Louise	Daughter	6
	Bepler, Doris	Daughter	4
	Bepler, Alice	Daughter	2
	Bepler, Beatrice	Daughter	1
63	Olinger, Charles	Head	44
	Olinger, Caroline	Wife	35
	Olinger, Ray	Daughter	15
	Olinger, Charles	Son	13
	Olinger, Allen	Son	12
	Olinger, Helen	Daughter	2
64	*Illegible*		
	Illegible		
	Illegible		

65	Hillebrand, August	Head	46
	Hillebrand, Maria	Wife	48

1910 Potomac Street Residents

44	Oller, John	Lodger	30
	Beresford, Thomas	Lodger	40
	Misor (?), Chester	Lodger	21
	Freikle, Augusta	Lodger	45
46	Britt, James	Head	54
	Britt, Rose	Daughter-in-law	27
	Britt, Wyllis	Granddaughter	2
47	Davis, H. L.	Head	33
	Davis, Mary	Wife	26
	Davis, Henry	Son	3
	Foster, Colin	Lodger	85
	Dale, Mary	Lodger	62
48	Kingsland, Olivia	Head	53
	Stein, Billie	Grandson	5
49	Barry, Susan	Head	45
	Eadon (?), Celia	Sister	38
	Eadon (?), Richard	Brother	19
	Martin, Rosa	Lodger	33
	Glasby, Catherine	Lodger	28
	Leary, Mary	Lodger	35
	Leary, Elvira	Lodger	21
	Bingham, Laura	Lodger	35
50	Wilson, O.	Head	37
	Wilson, Cornely	Wife	34
	Anderson, Hilda	Lodger	44
	Anderson, Ellen	Lodger	21
	Echland, August	Lodger	24
	Johnson, Alvin	Lodger	21
51	Bennet, Margaret	Head	45
	Berlin, Charles	Lodger	60
	Berlin, Mrs. Charles	Lodger	37
	Geeman (?), E. A.	Lodger	26
	Denson, Charles	Lodger	26
52	McCutchan, Charles	Head	35
	McCutchan, Annie	Wife	30
	McGowan, Marion	Lodger	23
53	Coffee, Edward	Head	41
	Coffee, Fernanda	Wife	38
	Coffee, Stanley	Son	13
	Coffee, Marshall	Son	11
	Coffee, Russell	Son	5
54	Snow, Harvey W.	Head	64
	Snow, Mary J.	Wife	60

	Name	Relation	Age
	McMurray, James	Head	80
	McMurray, Elizabeth	Wife	70
55	Aver, William	Head	42
	Aver, Virginia	Wife	37
	Aver, Vernan	Son	18
	Aver, Carlton	Son	17
56	Huntington, Pliny C.	Head	42
	Huntington, Adella M.	Wife	38
	Huntington, Cecil G.	Son	15
	Huntington, Helen	Daughter	14
	Huntington, Martha	Mother	84
	Forde, Ella	Servant	42
57	Aver, Frank	Head	47
	Aver, Ida	Wife	40
	Aver, Oswald	Son	21
	Aver, Rena	Daughter	18
59	Crosby, Patrick	Head	74
	Crosby, Rose	Daughter	30
	Crosby, Margaret	Daughter	25
60	Silley, Curtis W.	Head	27
	Silley, Emma R.	Wife	23
	Silley, Ralph C.	Son	1
61	Hernse, Harry	Head	33
	Hernse, Helen	Wife	31
	Hernse, Helen	Daughter	8
	Hernse, Grant	Brother	22
63	Olinger, Charles	Head	53
	Olinger, Caroline	Wife	44
	Olinger, Ray	Daughter	24
	Olinger, Allen	Son	21
	Olinger, Helen	Daughter	12
64	Bauer, Joseph	Head	51
	Bauer, Louise	Wife	49
65	McMurray, Milton	Head	45
	McMurray, Gertrude	Wife	40
	McMurray, Florence	Daughter	13
	McMurray, Ruth	Daughter	8
66	Gratto (?), Richard	Head	79
	Gratto (?), Katherine	Wife	73
	Nicol (?), Dora	Daughter	25
	Nicol (?), William Z.	Son-in-law	30
	Nicol (?), William G.	Grandson	1
	Hornbeck, Francis	Servant	19
67	Peterson, Neads	Head	44
	Peterson, Elizabeth	Wife	48
	Leasur, George	Lodger	41
	Leasur, Ivy	Lodger	14
	Leasur, Delila	Lodger	9

	Carr, William	Lodger	22
	Krouse, Edward	Lodger	22
	Johnson, John	Lodger	40
	Olson, Peter	Lodger	51
68	Cathcart, Charles R.	Head	33
	Cathcart, Gladys S.	Wife	27
	Cathcart, Gladys B.	Daughter	2
	Cathcart, Lena C.	Sister	25
	Cathcart, Luc H.	Brother	30
	Povelsen, Ingild	Lodger	49
	Warnock, William O.	Head	39
	Warnock, Fannie W.	Wife	35
69	Vintera, Vencel	Head	71
	Vintera, Marie	Daughter	36
	Urban, Joseph	Grandson	24
	Urban, Frank	Grandson	17
	Urban, Martha	Grandaughter	15
	Illegible	Lodger	41
	Illegible	Lodger	31
	Illegible	Lodger	31
	Lastufka, John	Head	44
	Lastufka, Emma (?)	Wife	49
	Ceran, Millie	Stepdaughter	26
	Ceran, Alma	Stepdaughter	25
	Ceran, Martha	Stepdaughter	23
	Ceran, Arthur	Stepson	17
69½	Coynton, Henry	Head	36
	Coynton, Edith	Wife	31
70	Arames (?), John H.	Head	56
	Arames (?), Myra	Wife	45
71-A	Berger, George	Head	49
	Berger, Jennie	Wife	48
72	*Unreported*		
73	Simpson, Harry	Head	40
	Simpson, Isabelle	Wife	34
	McCullough, Lillian	Sister-in-law	23
	Burhardt, Louise	Head	57
	Burhardt, Alvina	Daughter	33
	Eggers, Ferdinand	Lodger	60
74	Thompson, Elizabeth	Head	56
	Thompson, Elizabeth B.	Daughter	29
	Thompson, Frank S.	Son	20
	Thompson, James F.	Head	43
	Thompson, Eva D.	Wife	39
	Thompson, James D.	Son	5
	Thompson, Dorothy O.	Daughter	1
75	Levin, Moses	Head	60
	Levin, Annie	Wife	57
	Levin, David	Son	21

	Levin, Brodferd	Son	15
	Hayes, William	Head	39
	Hayes, Tillie	Wife	26
76	Sweasey, Frank R.	Head	34
	Sweasey, Anna B.	Wife	31
	McLeod, Carrie C.	Mother-in-law	62
77	Staurt, Peter	Head	26
	Staurt, Florence	Wife	21

1920 Potomac Street Residents

44	Canavan, Ellen	Head	64
	Canavan, William B.	Son	35
	Canavan, Evelyn	Daughter	24
	Clegg, Oscar A.	Lodger	63
	Spellane, Margaret H.	Lodger	26
	Lisner, William	Lodger	21
46	Pihlstrom, Axel	Head	49
	Pihlstrom, Millie E.	Wife	47
	Bergstrom, Norma	Stepdaughter	19
47	Dedrick, Earl George	Head	36
	Dedrick, Lula M.	Wife	35
	Dedrick, Marion L.	Daughter	7
	Dedrick, Elinore	Daughter	3
	Smith, Harley E.	Brother-in-law	27
48	Demarest, David M.	Head	36
	Demarest, Cora L.	Wife	34
49	Friedlander, Albert	Head	49
	Friedlander, Eva	Wife	49
	Friedlander, Ruth	Daughter	18
50	Quirk, Catherine	Head	75
	Quirk, William	Son	48
	Quirk, Elizabeth	Daughter	46
	Quirk, Mary	Daughter	33
	Quirk, Thomas F.	Son	29
51	Stonefield, Ida	Head	61
	Stonefield, Clare	Daughter	33
	Pfieffer, Edward	Lodger	66
	Oram, John H.	Lodger	37
	Miller, Dolly	Lodger	45
	Holman, Clarence A.	Lodger	53
	Carlson, Wanda	Lodger	45
52	Eakin, Robert	Head	43
	Eakin, Lillian	Wife	45
	Eakin, Roberta	Daughter	14
	Eakin, Harriet	Daughter	12
	Eakin, Marjorie	Daughter	9
	Eakin, Anita	Daughter	4
	Stamer, Amelia	Mother-in-law	64

53	Jacobi, David	Head	61
	Jacobi, Rosa	Wife	54
	Jacobi, Mory	Son	28
	Jacobi, Bertram	Son	23
54	Fisher, George	Head	39
	Fisher, Harriet	Wife	49
55	Aver, William	Head	52
	Aver, Virginia	Wife	47
	Aver, Carlton	Son	27
56	Court, John P.	Head	59
	Court, Ethel W.	Wife	39
	Mower, Orrin H.	Head	56
	Mower, Jennie	Wife	42
57	Aver, Frank	Head	53
	Aver, Ida	Wife	49
	Edwards, Tone	Lodger	32
59	Cannon, Steven F.	Head	35
	Cannon, Rose	Wife	35
60	Schmitz, Julius W.	Head	37
	Schmitz, Grelle W.	Son	7
	Schmitz, John L.	Son	6
	Roberts, Catherine	Housekeeper	63
61	Siewert, William	Head	41
	Siewert, Minnie	Wife	40
	Siewert, Lloyd	Son	17
	Siewert, Willard	Son	7
63	Olinger, Allen M.	Head	31
	Olinger, Mabel M.	Wife	30
	Olinger, Allen M., Jr.	Son	2
64	Paulson, Albert	Head	29
	Paulson, Rena	Wife	27
65	McMurray, Milton	Head	53
	McMurray, Gertrude	Wife	50
	McMurray, Ruth	Daughter	17
66	Holmari, Eliza	Head	56
	Holmari, Mildred	Daughter	28
	Holmari, Laurie	Daughter	27
	Wilkins, Sue	Head	26
	Manuell, Eva	Boarder	19
67	Peterson, Elizabeth J.	Head	64
	Snell, Irving B.	Head	64
	Snell, Susie A.	Wife	53
	Snell, Yulla E.	Daughter	8
	Stuart, William	Boarder	27
	Shankey, George W.	Boarder	52
	Miller, Tobias F.	Boarder	64
	Sullivan, Catherine	Boarder	35
	Harper, Elizabeth	Lodger	32

	Johnson, Emily	Lodger	29
	Johnson, Tinia (?)	Lodger	1
68	Smith, Fred	Head	34
	Smith, Orpha	Wife	30
	Smith, Jean	Daughter	9
	Smith, James A.	Son	6
	Vichey, Curtiss	Lodger	24
69	Novotny, Joseph	Head	41
	Novotny, Marie	Wife	46
	Vintera, Venger	Father-in-law	84
	Urban, Frank	Nephew	27
	Urban, Martha	Niece	25
	Rucera, Alois	Boarder	51
	Lastufka, John	Head	58
	Lastufka, Anna (?)	Wife	54
69½	*Unreported*		
	Unreported		
	Rimpy, Carl N.	Son	17
70	Armes, Mira	Head	54
	Head, Ella	Sister	67
	Murray, Gertrude	Boarder	32
71	Kahl, Franklin	Head	35
	Kahl, Hazel	Wife	30
	Kahl, Walter	Son	6
	Kahl, Clarence	Son	5
71-A	Welch, John	Head	45
	Welch, Johanna	Wife	42
	Welch, John T.	Son	13
72	Danielson, Carl T.	Head	50
	Danielson, Emily	Wife	42
	Danielson, Isabela	Daughter	16
	Killian, Phillip	Head	29
	Killian, Agnes	Wife	24
	Killian, Phissis	Daughter	3
	Killian, Phillip	Son	
73	Leonard, Edward H.	Head	55
	Leonard, Elizabeth T.	Wife	50
	Leonard, Joseph E.	Son	4
73-A	Plover, Ida	Head	53
	Plover, Charles	Son	29
74	Lurch, Edward	Head	51
	Lurch, Clara	Wife	51
	Lurch, Matilda	Mother	73
	Erickson, Emery E.	Head	33
	Erickson, Amelda	Wife	29
	Flanagan, Amelda	Stepdaughter	10
75	Condow, Rebecca	Head	53
	Condow, Edith	Daughter	14

	Hughes, Ruth	Daughter	22
	Hughes, Jean	Granddaughter	2
	Booth, Ruby	Granddaughter	7
	Furley, Fred	Son-in-law	30
	Furley, Frances	Daughter	18
	Trimel (?), Jacob	Head	58
75-A	Preast, Charles	Head	45
	Preast, Amelia	Wife	35
	Preast, Lieda	Daughter	6
76	Sweasey, Frank	Head	45
	Sweasey, Barbara A.	Wife	42
	McCloud, Caroline	Mother-in-law	72
	James, Jack	Head	31
	James, Agnes	Wife	29
	James, Dorothy	Daughter	2

1930 Potomac Street Residents

The 1930 census of Potomac Street was very poorly conducted. The handwriting of the census-taker is frequently difficult to decipher and she often crossed-out and wrote-over names and addresses, thereby making it difficult (if not impossible) to read them. In addition, she failed to include six (possibly seven) households. The following is my best rendering of the names of residents who lived on Potomac Street at the time of the 1930 census.

44	Rommerdahl, Canute (?)	Head	35
	Rommerdahl, Violet	Wife	29
	Raber, John	Lodger	42
	Crane, Arthur B.	Lodger	35
	Andzian (?), Bazen	Lodger	35
	Maggs, Herbert	Lodger	68
46	*Unreported*		
47	Davis, Elbert	Lodger	26
	Sargent, Glen	Lodger	30
48	Crawford, Carl E.	Head	52
	Crawford, Vera S.	Wife	38
49	*Unreported*		
50	Moore, Judson S.	Head	32
	Moore, Mary E.	Wife	33
	Moore, George W.	Son	9
51	Kuner, Ralph	Head	71
	Kuner, Bertha	Sister	72
52	Eakin, Sillian (?)	Head	53
	Eakin, Roberta S.	Daughter	24
	Eakin, Harriet A.	Daughter	22
	Eakin, Marjorie J.	Daughter	19
	Eakin, Anita I.	Daughter	14

53	Butcher, William B.	Head	60
	Butcher, Adriean (?)	Wife	61
	Butcher, William	Son	*Illegible*
	Butcher, Leslie	Son	*Illegible*
54	Spurgun, Gritta	Head	54
	Spurgun, Clarence D.	Son	25
	Spurgun, Buddy	Son	19
55	Avers, William	Head	62
	Avers, Virginia L.	Wife	57
	Avers, Carleton L.	Son	27
	Reynolds, *Illegible*	Daughter-in-law	52
56	Quigley, Chester	Head	32
	Quigley, Ella S.	Wife	19
	Gray, Hilly (?)	Mother-in-law	50
	Hunnigan, Pearl	Sister-in-law	13
57, 77, or 51? *(Illegible)*			
	Clancy (?), Christen	Head	47
	Christensen, Otto	Roomer	26
	Klein, Ella	Lodger	27 (?)
57	Sutherland, Annie	Head	40
	Sutherland, Bruce	Son	7
59	*Unreported*		
60	Chasten, Burford	Head	38
	Chasten, Rose J.	Wife	34
	Chasten, Burford	Son	16
	Chasten, Vincent	Son	14
61	Siewert, Edward L.	Head	40
	Siewert, Maude E.	Wife	29
	Siewert, Robert E.	Son	8
	Dunlea, Dennie P.	Boarder	50
63	Olinger, Allen	Head	41
	Olinger, Mable	Wife	39
	Olinger, Allen M., Jr.	Son	12
64	Girein, Paul S.	Head	40
	Girein, Evelyn	Wife	35
	Girein, Paul Jr.	Son	6
	Girein, *Illegible*	Son	2
	Girein, Doris	Daughter	9 mos.
65	Rohde, Arthur	Head	52
	Rohde, Mary	Wife	48
66	Moner (?), Orrin H.	Head	66
	Moner (?), Jennie E.	Wife	54
67	Peterson, Elizabeth	Head	68
	Illegible	Roomer	27
	Harper, Elizabeth	Roomer	30
	Connor, Mary	Roomer	45
	Portochnich, Blas (?)	Roomer	55

68	*Unreported*		
69	Novotny, Joseph	Head	51
	Novotny, Marie	Wife	*Illegible*
	Vintera, Venger	Father-in-law	*Illegible*
69-A	Lastufka, John O.	Head	54
	Lastufka, Emma	Wife	69
70	Biedenbach, Fred	Head	48
	Biedenbach, Elizabeth	Wife	46
	Biedenbach, Ralph O.	Son	23
	Biedenbach, Elizabeth A.	Daughter	21
	Biedenbach, Elsie	Daughter	18
71	Kahl, Franklin J.	Head	45
	Kahl, Hazel P.	Wife	40
	Kahl, Walter F.	Son	16
	Kahl, Clarence L.	Son	15
72	*Unreported*		
73	Leonand, Edward	Head	65
	Leonand, Joseph	Son	20
	Illegible, Anna	Roomer	40
73-A	Standart, Claude	Head	22
	Standart, Daisy Irene	Relative	40
74	Paasche, Orville	Head	30
	Paasche, Emma	Wife	27
	Schmose (?), Karl	Lodger	44
74	Wood, *Illegible*	Head	52
	Illegible	Son	25
	Wormell, Kate	Mother	75
75	Ommill, Jacob	Head	69
75-A	Giragirty (?), Clarence	Head	44
	Giragirty (?), Catheline	Wife	36
76	Kelly, Lyman S.	Head	73
	Kelly, Alice	Wife	50
	Hope, Nelson M.	Lodger	65
77	*Unreported*		
82	*Unreported*		
84	Omand, William	Head	31
	Omand, Myrtle	Wife	27
	Omand, Harold	Son	9
	Omand, Muriel	Daughter	8
86	Ducey (?), Peter	Head	65
	Ducey (?), Mary F.	Sister	68
Illegible	Crockett, Joseph	Head	50
	Crockett, Laura M.	Wife	44
	Crockett, Frances	Daughter	4
Illegible	Mecchia, Louis J.	Lodger	32
	Blackburn, Albert	Lodger	44

1940 Potomac Street Residents

44	Edith M. Winstanley	Head	61
46	Missak Kafeyan	Head	51
	Elmasas (?) Kafeyan	Wife	40
	Richard Kafeyan	Son	10
	Caroline Kafeyan	Daughter	6
47	Emma Conboie	Head	50
	Joseph Conboie	Husband	63
	Ellen Donling	Roomer	79
	Emily Petersen	Roomer	82
48	Svend Noble	Head	33
	Louise Noble	Wife	28
	James Noble	Son	7
49	Lavinia C. Marstin	Head	71
	Lillian J. Marstin	Sister	70
	Rose Ann Collapy	Roomer	65
	Nicholas Duffy	Roomer	48
50	Mearditch Koozoomian	Head	64
	Serpooli Koozoomian	Wife	55
	Rose Koozoomian	Daughter	26
	George Koozoomian	Son	23
	Paul Koozoomian	Son	21
51	John H. Oram	Head	58
	Zilpa Oram	Wife	57
	Jean Oram	Daughter	21
	Hazel Trail	Niece	14
	Ella Klein	Roomer	70
	Betty Reinera	Roomer	65
	Edward Connolly	Roomer	38
	Mike Lehner	Roomer	49
	Ella Becker	Roomer	60
	Julia Gasliner	Roomer	59
52	Arev H. Enjaian	Head	60
	Artemis Enjaian	Wife	42
	Raymond Enjaian	Son	13
	Rudolph Enjaian	Son	10
53	William A. Butcher	Head	70
	Eldrifien F. Butcher	Wife	71
53	John Linck	Head	46
	Timothy Rabbitte	Roomer	45
54	Theodore Schroder	Head	34
	Ann L. Schroder	Wife	31
	Margaret Schroder	Daughter	8
55	Mary Ritter	Head	52
	Jesse W. Ritter	Son	13
55	Gerald Portilla	Head	35
	Marian Portilla	Wife	25

	Robert Portilla	Son	1
56	Orin H. Mower	Head	76
	Jennie E. Mower	Wife	65
	Fred L. Pohl	Head	47
	Freda B. Pohl	Wife	53
59	Stephen F. Cannon	Head	60
	Henrietta Schwanen	Roomer	46
60	Emma Keller	Head	68
	Elvera Keller	Daughter	41
61	Axel Barkstrom	Head	64
	Emelia Barkstron	Wife	67
61-A	Anna M. Bente	Head	46
	Marie C. Carlson	Co-head	47
63	*Unreported*		
64	John R. Bolton	Head	68
	Hetty Bolton	Wife	63
65	Irving O'Neill	Head	33
	Eileen O'Neill	Wife	29
	Daniel I. O'Neill	Son	2
	George T. O'Brien	Brother-in-law	41
66	Charles Harris	Head	53
	Martha Harris	Wife	52
	Evelyn Casey	Daughter	24
	Edward Casey	Son-in-law	28
	Mary Gethian	Roomer	60
	Caroline Harvey	Roomer	47
67	Elizabeth Petersen	Head	85
67	Irvine Solberg	Head	49
	Agnes Solberg	Wife	48
	James Wallace	Roomer	46
68	Anton Polivka	Head	42
	Olga Polivka	Wife	41
	Charles Polivka	Son	21
	Marian Hinde	Daughter	20
	Kathleen Polivka	Daughter	18
	Frank Polivka	Son	15
	Dorthea Polivka	Daughter	9
	Donald Hinde	Grandson	1
69	Sarah E. Weir	Head	75
	Donald Weir	Grandson	20
69½	Antone Tonnessen	Head	49
	Berglit (?) Tonnessen	Wife	44
	Bernard Tonnessen	Son	14
69½	Danield Petersen	Head	39
	Ruth Petersen	Wife	35
69½	Mary E. Begin	Head	60

70	Fred Biedenbach	Head	58
	Elizabeth Biedenbach	Wife	56
	Ralph Biedenbach	Son	33
	Elsie Biedenbach	Daughter	29
71-A	Robert Anderson	Head	35
	Alice R. Anderson	Wife	29
	Betty Anderson	Daughter	11
	Emma Jane Anderson	Daughter	10
	Dorothy A. Anderson	Daughter	9
	E. Robert Anderson	Son	1
72	Bruce Belieu	Head	20
	Carmen Belieu	Wife	20
73	Jim Owens	Head	50
	Lillian Owens	Wife	38
	James W. Owens	Son	21
73-A	Jacob Immel	Head	79
74	Gus Sele	Head	57
	Bessie Hood	Housekeeper	44
74	Bert Velpa	Head	32
	Helen Velpa	Wife	24
	Arthur Velpa	Son	8
75	Albert Hopkins	Head	67
	Florence Hopkins	Wife	58
75-A	Franklin H. Graebers	Head	59
76	Robert Burrows	Head	27
	Leana Burrows	Wife	27
76	Jalana (?) Archibault	Head	42
	Alpha Archibault	Wife	41
	Elliott Bressler	Stepson	15
76	Ralph Bowen	Head	48
	Rossi Bower	Wife	49
77	*Unreported*		
82	*Unreported*		
84	Josephine Von Moos	Head	64
	Walter Von Moos	Grandson	16
86	Mary Darcey	Head	79

Appendix Four

1954 Potomac Street Residents

This list of Potomac Street residents is taken from *The San Francisco, Bayshore, Brisbane, Colma and Daly City Street Address Telephone Directory* that was published in September 1954 by the Pacific Telephone and Telegraph Company of San Francisco. Some residences had more than one telephone listed whereas others had none.

44	Mrs. R. C. Peddecord	63	Patrick Clarke
44-A	Zvi Danenberg	65	Irving D. O'Neill
46	Robert Colin	67	Mrs. Lena Mora
48	Olive M. MacDonald	68	Ramon Landron
50	Joseph Le Blanc	68	Frank H. Welch
53	Paul B. Schellhammer	69	O. L. Vanaksdell
53	Warren T. Schellhammer	69½	Glenn W. Kading
54	James E. Reed	69½	Minna Marin
55	Les Butcher	70	Edward Douglas
55	Mrs. Anna Gilfillan	72	Herman Brunmeier
55	John P. O'Neill	73	Elmo Ollison
56	Mrs. Agnes Todd	74	John J. Callicotte
57	Miss A. Casillas	76	Catherine Rios
59	Vicente Diala	77	Albert Sanchez
60	W. J. Wilken	82	Frank DiGiorno
61	Jens Strom	84	Anatol Kasatkin
61-A	Charlotte L. Ehling	86	Alessandro Cusin

1964 Potomac Street Residents

This list of Potomac Street residents is taken from *The Street Address Directory, San Francisco 1964* published by the Pacific Telephone and Telegraph Company. Some residences had more than one telephone listed whereas others had none.

44	D. Emerson	67	Leon Dilley
47	Robert Sundberg	67	Joe Ressemann
48	Corrine Taylor	67	Arnold H. Seibel
49	John D. Krueger	68	Buck Walter
51	M. Forman	69	Fred Lewis
51-A	Paul E. Bond	69½	Madora Towner
52	Diana G. Anderson	69½	Artis Smith
53	James Betton	70	Patricia A. Douglas
55-2	Roy Brown	71-A	Claiona H. Anderson
55-3	Marion Wright	73-B	Roscell Fisher
59	Albert F. Laureto	75-2	J. M. Molloy
60	Gloria Wilken	76-5	A. Klempner
61	Jens Strom	76-7	Mrs. Lee Jackson
61-A	Ethel Ige	82	John C. Bland
63	Mary W. Reed	84	Dorothy Chavez
64	Jeanette Trammell	86	Eutelia Herron
65	Nena Fontanilla		

Appendix Six
Memorial Piece for Mrs. Smith
by
Tanya Joyce

San Francisco Bay Area painter and poet Tanya Joyce lived at 47 Potomac Street from 1972 to 1984. Her studio overlooked Duboce Park where she spent much time walking her dog and exploring the park. She loved the neighborhood, and some of its people and places appear in her poetry.

"Memorial Piece for Mrs. Smith"[46] was written by Tanya after the tragic death of Mrs. Marjorie Smith who was murdered in her car on Christmas Eve 1979. She and her husband lived on nearby Pierce Street but they owned the building next door to the flat where Tanya lived. Longtime residents of Potomac Street will recognize many of the names mentioned in the poem as people who lived on the street at that time. Other poems by Tanya Joyce with Duboce Park settings appear in her books *A Sampler of Poems* and *Celestial Animals*.

MEMORIAL PIECE FOR MRS. SMITH

Green rain. San Francisco Christmas
Green this morning
In the rain
Marc brought back the Santa suit
Red and white velour bounced color at the green
Grass of the park.

Lorraine and Sylvia
On their ways to church this morning
Monday rainy
End to the year.

On Christmas Eve at ten p.m.
Our neighbor, Mrs. Smith,
According to the coroner,
Was shot.
Found in her car
Shot in the head
Heading toward church
For midnight services.

On Christmas Day in the afternoon,
Doug's brother
Beaten and robbed
Returning home from Doug and Tony's
Open house. Bright fires
In seven marble fire places, just restored,
Two Christmas trees all glowing and
Doug's brother beaten and robbed
As we welcomed foreign visitors
To our lovely, inexplicable
City.

Sonya said at the open house
For neighbors on the block
She was afraid
To walk the length of the park.
We teased her, felt she was plagued by
Groundless fears. It was her mother,
Mrs. Smith, shot in the head
Heading toward midnight services.

The little granddaughter, Sonya's child,
Her hair done up in ribbons
Brightly bobbing in the back seat
Of Sonya's car this morning on the way
To the funeral.

The wake was yesterday as,
Bright and bobbing, we waved to Sylvia and Lorraine
Heading toward the church. I knew they were
On their way to services by the somber clothes
They wore. None of their usual bright purples, but
Brown vests, black skirts, and white blouses
For the choir. Mrs. Smith
Shot in the head on Christmas Eve.
We waved, bright and bouncing,
On our way to New Year's,
Full of parties, full of friends, and Mrs. Smith,
Shot in the head.

Harry had said how he liked Mrs. Smith,
Told Sonya under the bright lights
Of Christmas, overlooking the park,
Where Sonya was afraid to walk.

It has not been published in the paper
Where Mrs. Smith was shot, whether the car
They found her in was moved before
Or after the shooting. Our hallway rug
Still wet from Christmas party drinks spilled
As we kissed good by to friends flying home
From lovely
San Francisco.

Gloria, green and gold Gloria, returning
In the rain from shopping now has lived here
All her life. Grates and metal over his windows now
An iron gate across the porch
For protection, a single woman
Caring for her ailing mother. No dogs
To guard her house. Overlooking the park
At the Christmas party, Gloria, Sylvia, and I
Laughing over the children Donald, Philip, Sebastian,
Benjamin, Lucy, and Deniseia; Charles, Dedrik, and Zeppie,
All asleep across the street. Their parents
Tiptoed out and tiptoed in alternating eggnog and
Parental protection at home across the street.

Thinking these thoughts, walking the dog
In the green rain of San Francisco,
Foggy pines and eucalyptus up the hill, looking
The same way I had looked uphill the day
Our mayor was shot
And killed, and our supervisor the only one
Who ever answered us at City Hall—
Was shot and killed. He represented
District Five. District Five was
All of us on the block, and in the park,
And Mrs. Smith, shot in the head,
Heading toward Christmas services.

Notes

1   San Francisco Board of Supervisors, 1909.

2   Robbins.

3   San Francisco Board of Supervisors, 1909.

4   *San Francisco Chronicle,* 1900, 9.

5   Olinger.

6   *San Francisco Chronicle,* 16 August 1900.

7   *San Francisco Call.*

8   Olinger.

9   Publications Department.

10 Robbins.

11 Robbins.

12 Publications Department.

13 *San Francisco Register of Voters,* 1912.

14 *San Francisco Register of Voters,* 1920.

15 San Francisco Board of Supervisors, 1927.

16 *San Francisco Chronicle,* 1928, 1.

17 *San Francisco Register of Voters,* 1930.

18 Etkin, 11.

19 San Francisco Gate.

20 *The Point,* 1996, 2-3.

21 *San Francisco Register of Voters,* 1940.

22 Benet.

23 *San Francisco Register of Voters,* 1944.

24 *San Francisco Register of Voters,* 1950.

25 Diala.

26 *San Francisco Chronicle,* 1957, 6.

27 Doss.

28 mitchtv.

29 *San Francisco Progress.*

30 *San Francisco Examiner,* 1970, 52.

31 doudou1.

32 *San Francisco Chronicle*, 28 March 1975; *San Francisco Chronicle*, 29 March 1975.

33 *San Francisco Chronicle*, 19 June 1975; *San Francisco Examiner*, 1975.

34 Jennings.

35 Bartlett.

36 Levering 1978, 7.

37 Levering 1977, 1978; Burns; Giteck; Butler and Evans; Butler.

38 Butler.

39 Hemphill.

40 Levering 1977, 4.

41 *San Francisco Chronicle*, 1980.

42 Nimmo.

43 Rust, 8.

44 Howe, B1.

45 Van Derbeken.

46 Joyce 2006, 53-55.

Bibliography

Bartlett, Robert. Cops Sweep S.F. Block 54 Arrested. *San Francisco Chronicle*, 3 November 1977, 1, 30.

Benet, Jane. A Market Born of Shortages. *San Francisco Chronicle*, 13 June 1979.

Burns, Jerry. Gay Speculators Worry Black Group. *San Francisco Chronicle*, 6 February 1979.

Butler, Katy. Gays Who Invested in the Black Areas. *San Francisco Chronicle*, 1 September 1979, 4.

Butler, Katy and Gwendolyn Evans. Gay Migration into Black Neighborhoods. *San Francisco Chronicle*, 1 September 1979, 1, 5.

Diala, Ed. Letter to H. Arlo Nimmo. 4 January 2010.

Doss, Margot Patterson. A Walk in a Much-Used Park. *San Francisco Sunday Chronicle*, 5 August 1962, 16-17.

doudou1. Comments. Neighborhood Mirrors S. F.'s Evolution by Carl Nolte. *San Francisco Chronicle*. 3 January 2010. www.sfgate.com.

Etkin, Coral. Duboce Park: A Home for the Neighborhood. Unpublished manuscript. Author's Collection. 1982.

Giteck, Lenny. Speculators and the Gay Housing Boom. *San Francisco Examiner*, 20 November 1978, 21.

Hemphill, Paul Wally Baptiste. *San Francisco Examiner*, 11 October 1976, 21.

Howe, Kenneth. High Aspirations in the Lower Haight. *San Francisco Chronicle*, 24 October 1994, B1, B3.

Jennings, Duffy. Inside the Big Raid. *San Francisco Chronicle*, 4 November 1977, 1.

Joyce, Tanya. *A Sampler of Poems*. Concord: Small Poetry Press, 2005.

_____ *Celestial Animals*. Concord: Small Poetry Press, 2006.

Levering, Bob. Mining Gold at Haight and Fillmore. *San Francisco Bay Guardian*, 24 March 1977, 4-6.

_____ The Lavendering of the Haight/Fillmore. *San Francisco Bay Guardian*, 23 March 1978, 6-7.

mitchtv. Gypsies, Tramps and Thieves installment 3. democraticunderground. com. 31 January 2008.

Nimmo, H. Arlo. Journal of an Old House. Unpublished manuscript. Author's Collection. 1972-2007.

Olinger, Ray L. Letter to Joseph Gross. Author's Collection. 1965.

The Point. Mrs. Oram's Kitchen. February 1996, 2-3.

Publications Department. *Dedication to Health: A History of the Ralph K. Davies Medical Center.* San Francisco: Ralph K. Davies Medical Center, 1974.

Robbins, Millie. '06 at German Hospital. *San Francisco Chronicle,* 13 April 1965, 15.

Rust, Marion. Higher Living in the Lower Haight. *The Calendar,* April 1987, 8-9.

San Francisco, Bayshore, Brisbane, Colma and Daly City Street Address Telephone Directory. September 1954. San Francisco: The Pacific Telephone and Telegraph Company, 1954.

San Francisco Blue Book. San Francisco: Charles C. Hoag, 1911-1927.

San Francisco Board of Supervisors. *Real Estate Owned by the City and County of San Francisco and Historical Data Relating to Same, With Citations From Decisions of the Superior, Supreme and Federal Courts in Relation to Land Titles Vested in the Municipality.* San Francisco: A. Carlisle Company, 1909.

_____ *Journal of Proceedings.* Volume 22, No. 1. San Francisco: Recorder Printing and Publishing Company, 1927.

San Francisco Call. Duboce Park is now for the City. 10 September 1900, 2.

San Francisco Chronicle. Colonel Duboce, of the First California, Dead. 16 August 1900, 1.

_____ Dedication of Duboce Park. 10 September 1900, 9.

_____ New Service Gives Direct Route from Bay to Beach. 22 October 1928, 1.

_____ New Recreation Center Opens. 21 December 1957, 6.

_____ Stick of Dynamite in Sunset Tunnel. 28 March 1975.

_____ More Sticks of Dynamite in Tunnel. 29 March 1975.

_____ Spectacular Fire in S.F. Apartments. 19 June 1975, 1, 22.

_____ Use of Herbicide Upsets Neighbors. 28 June 1980, 3.

San Francisco Examiner. Safety Fence for Duboce. 14 August 1970, 52.

_____ Duboce Fire Threatens a Block. 19 June 1975.

San Francisco Gate. *San Francisco Chronicle.* 13 May 2012.

San Francisco Progress. Groundbreakers. 15 April 1970, 1.

San Francisco Register of Voters. 1912, 1920, 1930, 1940, 1944, 1950, and 1994.

San Francisco Water Department Records. Potomac Street.

Street Address Directory. San Francisco. 1964. San Francisco: The Pacific Telephone and Telegraph Company, 1964.

United States Census. 1900, 1910, 1920, 1930, and 1940.

Van Derbeken, Jaxon. Mission Star Slain "for his family's sins." *San Francisco Chronicle,* 17 February 2007, A1, A11.

H. ARLO NIMMO is Professor Emeritus of Anthropology at California State University East Bay. He has conducted anthropological research in Hawai`i and the Sulu Archipelago of the southern Philippines, and is the author of ten books and dozens of articles.

www.ingramcontent.com/pod-product-compliance
Lightning Source LLC
Chambersburg PA
CBHW071404280526
45787CB00001B/421